Trial by Combat

A Paratrooper of the 101st Airborne Division Remembers the 1944 Battle of Normandy

by

Thomas M. Rice

authorHOUSE™

1663 LIBERTY DRIVE, SUITE 200
BLOOMINGTON, INDIANA 47403
(800) 839-8640
WWW.AUTHORHOUSE.COM

© *2004 Thomas M. Rice*
All Rights Reserved.

No part of this book may be reproduced, stored in a retrieval system, or transmitted by any means without the written permission of the author.

First published by AuthorHouse 11/08/04

ISBN: 1-4184-9130-6 (sc)
ISBN: 1-4184-9129-2 (dj)

Library of Congress Control Number: 2004096056

Printed in the United States of America
Bloomington, Indiana

This book is printed on acid-free paper.

Dedication

Oh men of valor, who metamorphosed from sow's ears to silk purses, who pursued the hounds of hell in the killing fields of Operation Overlord, Normandy, June 6, to July 13, 1944, I hope you get to read this book before you die. You made it all possible by your gallantry while others simply, "jested at scars, who never felt a wound."

We was bad asses; we was bad bastards!

Men of valor, especially all of you who have lived to a point of death and leaped over it:[1] This book is for you.

---

[1] Pyle, Ernie, Ernie's War, pge.347.

Table of Contents

Dedication v
About the Author..ix
Foreword xi
Acknowledgments..xv
Chapter 1 My Teeming Brain..1
Chapter 2 As a Civilian - Coronado..9
Chapter 3 Induction, Army Style 21
Chapter 4 Basic Training Knocking the Civilian Out of Us........29
Chapter 5 Fort Benning - Jump School.................................39
Chapter 6 Camp Mackall-Advanced Training 51
Chapter 7 Overseas - England...69
Chapter 8 The Enemy 83
Chapter 9 Cross Channel - Low Angle of Attack 109
Chapter 10 The Jump - The Landing Flash - Thunder - Welcome 119
Chapter 11 Drop Zone - D Addeville, France.....................129
Chapter 12 Assembly For La Barquette Lock.....................137
Chapter 13 Capture Of Carentan...149
Chapter 14 The Longest Week Captain Robert H. Phillips Vice President Trust Company of Georgia 157
Chapter 15 D-Day Experiences Of Lieutenant Eugene D. Brierre..169
Chapter 16 D-day Experiences of S/Sgt. Myron G. Sessions June 6 - June 13, 1944 175
Chapter 17 The Pastures of Death Revisited 181
Bibliography 201

Thomas M. Rice, age 20, Coronado, California

About the Author

Thomas M. Rice was born August 15, 1921, in Coronado, California, of a naval aviation family. His father was killed in a military air crash in the Panama Canal Zone, 1934.

Tom graduated from Coronado High School in 1940, entered San Diego State College the same year, enlisted in the United States Army 1942 as a volunteer for the newly formed 501st Parachute Infantry Regiment. After basic training at Camp Toccoa, Georgia, he finished jump school at Fort Benning, Georgia, in 1943.

Staff Sergeant Thomas M. Rice fought in some of the major battles of World War II, including Normandy, Market-Garden, and the Battle of the Bulge. He made combat jumps in Normandy and Market-Garden. In Normandy he was wounded by shrapnel and caught a sniper's bullet in his left knee. At Bastogne during the Battle of the Bulge a bullet blasted his left leg just above the knee, and other bullets tore a four inch piece out of the radial bone just below the elbow of his right arm.

Military awards include 4 campaigns, Purple Heart with two Oak Leaf clusters, Two Invasion Arrows, Combat Infantry Badge, Bronze Star with cluster, Good Conduct Medal, French Fourregue, Belgium Lanyard and Parachutist Badge.

After combat operations, he finished college for his BA degree, earning a General Secondary Teaching Credential. He taught U.S. government, U.S. history and coached cross-country and track and field teams for forty-four years. He retired in 1984 and lives with his wife Barbara, a retired elementary school teacher.

Foreword

In early June, 1944, the battle-hardened veterans of the German 6th Parachute Regiment were well aware that the Allied invasion of Western Europe was imminent. They were stationed in the Normandy area of Fortress Europa and were not particularly worried about the coming battle. Chances were that the Allied forces would not begin their assault in their sector, and if they did, the green, untried American troops would be easy pickings for their elite unit whose creed was, "You must conquer or die... to you death or victory must be a point of honor."

However, shortly after midnight on June 6, in weather that had been so foul, the German high command being sure that no army in its right mind would attempt an assault on a fortified coast under such conditions, Thomas M. Rice and thousands of other "Screaming Eagles" of the 101st Airborne division parachuted into the night sky, and swooped down upon the Germans with a fury never before seen by the Nazi "supermen."

The terrified 6th Parachute Regiment, which had been led to believe that the Americans were nothing but pampered wimps, was suddenly wondering, "Who are these guys?" Or in James Mitchner's famous line: "Where did they get such men?" Days later a letter was found on one of the Germans which stated: "God help us! These Americans are even fiercer than the Russians."

All of this is a well- documented part of our history, but if any fool thinks that this struggle was a glorious affair, let them read *Trial By Combat*, Thomas M. Rice's account of his experiences leading up to and participating in the battle for Normandy.

In prose as simple and eloquent as the white crosses that mark the graves of fallen Americans all over the globe, Rice tells how he and his regiment were turned from carefree kids into the fierce warriors that sent the startled, demoralized Nazis into headlong retreat and final destruction. Rice doesn't sanitize or sensationalize his combat experiences; he tells us of the utter chaos of battle -- the terror, the carnage, the horror, the folly of war. The word "glory" is not found in Rice's, story, except on two occasions when he uses it ironically in reference to the foolish expectations of raw recruits. Words such as patriotism, courage, and honor are seldom written by Rice, but in the facts and eyewitness accounts presented here, we discover what genuine patriotism is, what courage consists of, and what a frightful price must be paid for honor.

This book is not ghost-written. Every word, every phrase, every sentence was meticulously fashioned by the author himself and carefully fitted into place. He has followed Shakespeare's advice to "Say what you feel, not what you ought to say."

<u>Trial By Combat</u> should be read by all Americans, and we ought to make it required reading for all politicians and media persons who have any influence on those who have the power to send Americans into battle.

But this book is not only fine reading for its instructional value alone. It is a fascinating, often thrilling look into the mind of one the heroes who fought so valiantly to free the world of the depravity of totalitarianism -- that had enslaved so many formerly free people. The battle for Normandy was a seminal event in the liberation of Europe. One can only imagine the thrill of hope that lifted the hearts the "huddled masses yearning to breathe free..." when they first heard of the Allied landings. A poignant example can be found in young Anne Frank's diary when she writes of how excited she and her family were when they received the joyful news.. The final defeat of the Nazi came too late for Anne Frank and too many other poor souls, but many millions of others survived to breathe the air of freedom because of the valor and suffering of extraordinary men like Thomas M. Rice and his fellow liberators. Their noble sacrifices will be remembered by civilized human beings " So long as men can breathe and eyes can see..." TGR

Acknowledgments

I am startled by the vast number of people, near and far, who have been invaluable in helping me assemble the materials from which this manuscript emerged. Several stand out. First, my wife, Barbara, who put up at home with the slow paced temperment of a 'first time writer' and sprinkled it with some patience, with some humor and with some directions. Second, S/Sgt Myron G. Sessions, who related detailed combat sequences about his parachute mis-drop in Normandy, June 6 - June 13, 1944. His adventures in <u>The Longest Week</u> of 'cops and robbers, Indians and cowboys' twenty miles behind German enemy lines. Third, Thomas G. Robinson, a high school English teacher of twenty-six years, who cajoled and tempered me to pick up a red hot pen, to melt away writer's block and directed me to trudge the steps to publication. I thank him for his wisdom and time spent. Fourth, James Heiner, a high school English teacher, who directed the removal of my grandiose sprinkling of commas and redesigned my sentence structure. I thank him for his enthusiasm and deligent attention to detail.

I acknowledge the efforts of Jhana Petersen who, in addition to being a daughter-in-law, provided multiple versions and ideas for the cover of this book, ultimately creating what I feel best interprets and satisfies both my vision and my word. I thank her for invaluable assistance and willingness to help guide me through this process.

Others who have helped me think back on my and their military service and remember the places we have been, the soldiers we have known and the battles we have fought are Lt. Eugene D. Brierre, Major Mike G. Sessions, PFC Hillel Rosenthal, Joanna McDonald and Jerry Radway. Their memory has caused me to return wistfully to the past and moved me to regret, desire, and sorrow of the realization of the eventuality of age and change. A special thank you to one 'young of heart' Erin Michele Millard who helped with enduring enthusiasm. Also a special thanks to Mary Ann Robinson, for without her amazing computer skills and hard work, I never could have prepared the many pictures that appear in this book. I would also like to thank Tommy Millard, Sally Patricia Robinson and Joseph D. Robinson for their help. TMR

Chapter 1

My Teeming Brain

*When I have fears that I may cease to be
Before my pen has gleaned my teeming brain...*
-- John Keats --

    Half a century after parachuting into Normandy, I think of war not as an academic endeavor on the foreign fields but as an emotional response to physical terror resulting from two combat parachute jumps behind enemy lines four wounds and five campaigns in Europe.

    As I write this the rusting carcasses of military machines still survive on the sandy and rock strewn beaches: Utah, Omaha, Juno, Sword, and Gold. The artillery pock-marked pastures have gradually returned to their natural state, moistened by the flood-tide of three Normandy rivers and numerous tributaries. The ruined German blockhouses are still surrounded by rusting serpentine barbed wire entanglements at Pointe Du Hoc. Some people used to call this the Field of Honor.

    Quickly my teeming brain flashes back to when the green leaves and the broken branches were still lying along the roadside ditches. The smell of rotting apples and pears, left unharvested on the ground, permeates the orchard, so immaculate. Concrete is shattered, power and telephone lines lie snarled, coils of copper wire crisscross the roads of vehicular and animal traffic. The gray powder-burned rims of bomb craters reveal soldier blood-stained soil and laying near by are dented steel helmets, broken rifles, scorched uniforms and unexploded military ordnance. The village reveals burned out tanks and splintered, overturned broken wooden carts. In the pastures the bloated carcasses of farm animals lie grotesquely with legs pointing skyward. The blackened crumbled walls of homes and barns, without roofs, are still smoldering above charred, ruined household furnishings. Fences and gates lie askew creakingly swinging in the evening breeze. From all this, one knows that the battle recently waged here has moved on its axis, reflecting an altered inhuman, scorched earth landscape. The staccato of barking military weapons has ceased. There is nothing but lifeless debris and the struggle of nature (sunshine, rain and flowers) to reconstitute itself while the darkness still reverberates in the minds of men who recently fought here. These scenes give testimony to the fact that there was once a Fortress Europa. If you ever wonder about the horrible cost of assaulting that fortress, remember that there are cemeteries in upper and lower Normandy where more than 9000 American heroes lie at rest.

Now my mind switches again and I am reminded that on June 6, 1944, at 12:00 A.M., along 7000 yards of French coastline (Utah, Omaha, Juno, Gold and Sword beaches) the door of freedom for the conquered nations finally swung open. It was their first moment of Liberty after years of oppression. In this book I will tell about my part in helping to force open that great door.

The idea of a life of action had attracted me all of my life, but my encounter with the 501st Parachute Infantry Regiment -- the pathos, the strangeness of that encounter-was more than an attraction; it was a revelation for in the crucible of my experiences: Normandy Invasion - Operation Overlord; Holland - Operation Market Garden; Ardennes, Belgium, Battle of the Bulge; and the Redoubt of Austria Yugoslavia, fashioned me into a creature far different than the carefree lad who grew up in a small, sleepy Southern California town.

This is a story of my indoctrination into four years of parachute army life, where I trained, how I trained, the equipment I used, and finally what I 'liberated' during combat. It is also a narrative about

Trial by Combat

soldierly feelings, about my ability to deal with the enemy close up and at a distance, seen and unseen.

It is a story of how I arrived on the continent of Europe- Normandy, France, and touched down in a field in darkness, not knowing where I was. I couldn't see the enemy, but I could hear him. I was trained to know what to do, but I still was wounded four times in battle. The only constant combat axiom is that combat is confusion; it is always total confusion on the battlefield.

I survived eleven months of combat with Company C, 501st Parachute Infantry Regiment of the famous 101 st Airborne Division- Screaming Eagles - which included five campaigns. During all of this activity, the army couldn't burn up or burn out my energies because they didn't know how.

I have retained numerous life-long experiences from my four years of military service. Some were crucial to combat survival, others were crucial to leadership development. It was the most informative time of my life.

At Camp Toccoa, Georgia, during the winter of 1942 to the spring of 1943, we all dressed alike, ate the same meals, spoke the same military language. We shared the same emotional and physical responses to rugged parachute training of uncertainties, to confusion of military discipline and military orders, many times over.[2]

We were being molded and sent into combat as killing machines to be able to deal with the entire scope of emotional and physical endurance of combat which would eventually be placed before us until the war ended. But unlike our weapons we could think and feel. We shared laughter at times of joy and fellowship at times of boredom. We felt like crying when we felt the severe pain of cold sleeplessness and hunger. We shared the same dangers, the same sorrows, and the confusion of battle orders.

At times, we stood at attention in mutual fear, tense in muscles and frozen in intellect, in different ways, as military commands like exploding bombs and artillery from field exercises rained down upon us seeking to pulverize and atomize us as officers registered us in their gun sights.[3]

---

2 Sefton, William, My War, pge.10.
3 Orfalea, Gregory, Messengers of the lost Battalion, pge. xix.

This was the origin of the development of the 'brotherhood' for airborne soldiers from the training fields at camp Toccoa Georgia, to the pastures of death at Camp Mourmelon, France, in the European combat zone, 1942-1944.

We did the bulk of airborne fighting and along the way we became buddies forging a unique 'friendship' by baring our souls to one another as the relationships grew stronger. We experienced a trust that would be rare in civilian life. This friendship was the only gift to one another as a reward for enduring experiences both horrifying and defining. This was the cement for equality trust and a fierce kind of loyalty and pride that led us to become excellent soldiers. Once we shared these peaceful qualities, we cherished them.

We saw things and we did things that gave us a life-time of nightmares and smoldering guilt. Everywhere we went and everything we did shaped our perspective. For us the war never ends.

This complex blend of physical and mental combat teamwork was the main reason why we were successful in Normandy, even though we were surrounded by death and destruction that left us with a feeling of subdued rage directed toward the enemy.

We were stripped to a common denominator with all of our company friends and introduced to the basic elements of military lore. In a broad sense the army was "trying to wash and knock the civilian out of us raw recruits." We were to jump from sows' ears to silk purses.

I soon discovered that morale and espirit de corps waxes and wanes with life in the barracks and in the field as we gained experiences through challenges and exercise of leadership.

It wasn't very easy to learn that you should never underestimate the intelligence of your squad, the other squad leaders and your platoon officers, that the first combat is a traumatic experience, alone or in a group. You must realize that you have to move quickly against the enemy, and that there will always be casualties in combat.

The only effective shield against mental and emotional combat stress is a firm conviction that there is a supreme being, that you are in prime physical condition, that your buddies can be relied upon to

Trial by Combat

cover you in an engagement, and that you will give yourself first aid in an emergency and you accomplish your mission.

The object is to survive, that is the only way to win a war; force the enemy to make the sacrifices. In this way you hope to reduce the real danger to an inconvenience. You become an admired leader through sound judgment and good tactics. Don't give orders that you wouldn't execute yourself. A leader should be up front where the action is. Don't let confusion confound you into immobility because the country's fate lies in the hands of it's citizen soldiers. For in the clash of battle is found the final test of plans, training equipment and above all, the spirit of its fighting men, in units and as individuals[4]

Lord Acton said, " It is better to stay down where your fighting men stayed, close to the earth and terror, for the truth of war is there (not in the planning room), that is where solitary passionate human beings are, who have no other possession but their lives."

This is an account of the combat experiences that I had with the 501st Parachute Infantry Regiment during Operation Overlord-the invasion of Normandy, France, in 1944- at the foxhole level.

It is a story of how my Company C friends fought their hearts out on a strange plot of foreign soil, and of how many of my brave comrades gave their lives serving the country they loved.

Our commanders were kept busy trying to maintain the regimental strength of two thousand men in the course of four years. We had to replace nearly four thousand men during those years, but most of them were lost to us because of serious wounds or death.

The experience of visiting an American or German military cemetery will always draw my thoughts toward the battlefield, as I traveled with my buddies along the way. My physical and emotional senses will be overcome by compassion and sorrow for those soldiers interred there. I came to live out your courage and honor. As I silently walked through this guilt ridden cemetery at Colville Sur Mere (Omaha Beach), trying not to step on the grave sites, I searched the rows of comrade graves and stood by the ones that I knew and had known in combat. Softly and melodiously, carillons chimed the

---

4 Center of Military History, Utah Beach to cherbourgh, pges.100-12.

refrains of 'Yankee Doodle Dandy'. I place my right hand on one of the white crosses and my mind flashes back as I try to remember what these men were really like, in a symbolic act of praise. There are many qualities they had in common; qualities of energy, trust loyalty and a fierce determination to carry out their orders regardless of the consequences. I find myself making out a list of the qualities that characterized the combat soldiers I have known.

He volunteered for airborne service.

He saw the platoon officers as an ordinary men with higher test scores, more college education, ill-bred with a blossoming aptitude for leadership.

He developed a genuine dislike for small-mindedness and pettiness

His greatest desire was to survive the war.

He had developed a very special bond with his combat buddies.

He understood the long term effect of fear and exhaustion. Hatred of the enemy motivated him to revenge when he lost a squad member under fire.

He believed in god and preserved his sanity by prayer.

He knew that fear was real, but controllable.

He never became accustomed to death during and after combat.

He never made a front-line mistake by violating the elementary principles of infantry tectics.

He never fired his rifle unless he had engaged a target, always took advantage of cover and never froze up

He had developed the ability to function even when he was surrounded by death.

He never let a buddy down and always did his share.

He belonged to an elite fraternity of infantrymen who slept in the mud, killed his enemies, but tended the wounds of his buddies, and endured the pain and misery of constant exhaustion.

I pause in my list-making; then I give up, realizing that words and lists of words can't explain what these men were like, as I triumph over everything that has turned into gratitude.

This generation has gone from youth to adulthood, to middle age, and to old age but they were the rambunctious, high spirited kids of yesteryear who died in battle. What plays out in the minds of

Trial by Combat

us survivors is not guilt but grief and sorrow for the dead comrades who were never able to enjoy a long productive life.[5]

What else can be said? Thank you, my brothers, rest in peace, as each day and night becomes as silent as a grave.[6]

Pain makes man think thought makes man wise, and wisdom makes life endurable. Truth is so valuable that it is surrounded by a bodyguard of lies.

All of these images and thoughts tumble wildly through my mind as I prepare to write my story, but I am an orderly man by nature, and every story needs a beginning, so I will begin this one with my departure from my hometown on November 16, 1942.

---

5 McManus, John, The deadly Brotherhood, pges.334.
6 Tucker, Sandra, Parachute Soldier, Preface.

Chapter 2

As a Civilian - Coronado

Youth is beautiful
My lost Youth
Often I think of the beautiful town,
that is seated by the sea.
Often in thought I go up and down,
The pleasant streets of that old town
My youth comes back to me.
                    Author unknown

On a hot summer day in the city of Coronado, California, August 15, 1921, I was born. My father, Marcus S. Rice, was a veteran of the First World War and a naval warrant officer associated with naval aviation. Consequently we followed him around the globe to many fascinating places, where I experienced many exciting adventures. I was curious to learn about his experiences and the 1921 influenza epidemic. He volunteered to undergo hospitalization and experiment with garlic sandwiches as a possible cure. He didn't want to talk about it. It was easy to read the pain in his eyes.

I was faced with the fragility of life before my eleventh birthday on May 23, 1934. My father had been stationed in the Panama Canal

Zone at Coco Solo, on the Atlantic side of the Canal Zone. Officers of my father's squadron, VP-T3 came to our house. I remember it was a humid sunny day. They spoke quietly to my mother, Katherine and sister, Katherine, while I sat in my elementary school 6 th grade classroom. Before class was dismissed, two women came to inform the teacher of a tragedy. I was called out of the classroom and in the hall and was informed of what had happened to my father. They took me home and comforted my mother, who was in deep sorrow for the first time - the death of her 6 year old son Joseph, my brother, of double pneumonia, in Norfolk, Virginia. My father had been killed in an aircraft crash at Patilla Point, Bay of Panama, in the Canal Zone. He was forty-eight years old and at the nob end of his aviation career. One of the engines had failed after take-off and the amphibious plane smashed headlong into the Bay of Panama from three hundred feet altitude and sank in deep water. We were escorted to San Francisco, by a squadron officer, where my father was buried at the Presidio. As I looked at his flag -draped coffin I realized that I would never know this vibrant young man's history. The chronicle of his military experience in World War I was lost forever. Two long years later my mother received a letter from Admiral Ernest J. King, Chief of Naval Operations, which provided more details of my father's untimely death.

My mother, sister and I boarded the American President liner *President Lincoln* to San Francisco, California, and stayed with my father's mother. The ship voyage went smoothly until my sister disappeared. Mother was beside herself with grief. A little 2 year old on a big ship could be anywhere. Several tense hours passed as the crew searched for her. She was nowhere to be found. I was walking and looking near the railing of the ship. "Katherine, Katherine!", I called out. I caught a glimpse of something hanging over the ship's railing. It was Katherine. She had somehow climbed over the barrier and was leaning forward over the ship's side. She held on to the fencing and her little heels were locked in the scuppers. I put a death grip on her arms and shoulder and carefully pulled her to safety. Taking up a new role was going to be a tough schedule even after I dived into the ship's swimming pool and struck my head on the bottom, which knocked me unconscious for a moment. The cool water quickly brought me to my senses.

Returning to Coronado after a year in San Francisco, I finished junior high school and went to Coronado High School. My favorite subjects were ancient history, medieval history, modern history, English literature, algebra and mechanical drawing. Coronado High School had an excellent curriculum, oriented to the University of California system. Coronado pumped more graduating students into the military academies than any other high school in southern California, perhaps because there were many more military officers of all ranks and branches per capita than any other city in California.

The academic competition was stiff and the athletic teams, for the seasonal sports, were made up primarily from the same students. They were characterized as small in numbers and physical size but fast and intelligent. There was one coach for the seasonal sports (there was no one else). A baseball team wasn't fielded because there wasn't playing space. The student body of three hundred represented grades nine through twelve. Although I did well in the classroom, I found that my athletic skills allowed me to set several records in track and field -- one for the 3/4 mile and another for the mile run, which stood unbroken for ten years. I also played center on the championship basketball team. Receiving notoriety and friends from particitatiing in sports made it possible for me to be elected class president in my senior class.

The level of social activities was at a constant year-round whirl, both formal and informal. If you didn't have the appropriate accutrements you were at a distinct disadvantage. The Officer's Club at North Island Naval Air Station was a week-end rendezvous point as well as the Circus Room of the Hotel Del Coronado.

I can remember the day that Germany invaded Poland -- September 1, 1939 -- the principal of Coronado High School, during a hastily-called student body assembly, bade farewell to several foreign exchange students who had been called into service by their native countries. We listened to a radio broadcast telling of a *blitzkrieg.* Mr. Cutler, the principal said, "Before this is over, many of you will have been in it. "He was right, but I had to finish my four years of high school, and as a senior I had only one year to finish. I graduated in 1940 with a "well done" academic record.

After high school, I was accepted into San Diego State College as an engineering major. War had been declared during my first year in college. Because I felt continuing in school and receiving a degree would be more beneficial, I remained in college during 1941. As the months went by, I watched as the other college students went off to enlist in the military services of their choice. I viewed the newsreels of the Nazi regime creating havoc in Europe, and I realized I had to join the fight.

My last evening, in Coronado, was the most memorable one. The afternoon light faded into twilight on Monday, November 16, 1942. As I walked along the old familiar streets, I passed by houses of my old high school friends. The sidewalks seemed to roll up behind me. I wanted to infuse every aspect of my hometown upon my memory, each face, each doorway, each palm tree to remember this spectacular place and reminisce to my military buddies about its beauty.

No only did I drink in the ambience of this little town by the ocean on my last day, but I needed to relax, so I headed toward the Coronado motion picture theater. *Blue Lagoon* starring Dorothy Lamour and Harry James was playing. As I continued down the streets my thoughts jumped to the future. Tomorrow I was going to commit myself to the United States Army. I was a volunteer to the new parachute infantry regiments. I hadn't been in an airplane let alone jumped out of one, relying on a nylon chute to open and carry me through the sky looking for a safe landing spot back on earth.

Why was I doing this? Beyond the pressure of the war effort, I actually thought this might be a great adventure. I was a risk-taker. I had the athletic ability, and I was a competitor. Also I couldn't help noticing that the Navy ensigns, with their pair of golden aviator wings pinned on their white uniforms, had captured the hearts of all of the girls in town. The ensigns had a uniform, gold wings, money, wheels and the approval of the girls' parents. I wanted a pair of silver wings as well, even if it meant gaining them by way of a parachute. Before the war was over I had two invasion stars on my parachute wings.

Trial by Combat

My attention was jolted back to the moment when I saw a gigantic sheet of orange - blue flame belch forth from the house at 901 Ninth Street, as I crossed the street, looking back over my left shoulder. I heard a sharp crackling sound of rolling thunder, and the front part of the roof blew off of the house. Shards of glass and pieces of window frame flew out horizontally, expanding the killing zone. What was left of the curtains, shredded from the force of the blast, flapped and glowed from the scorching flames. It was a brilliant and terrifying image of household destruction. Surprisingly little smoke was seen or smelled; it happened so quickly. The roof crashed back into place, and an ominous silence prevailed. The shadows of the trees in the yard danced about like escaping inhabitants. The sky was a perfect black after the brilliant pyrotechnics. I ran to the front door to pull it open. The door was locked and bolted; it wouldn't budge. Someone must be inside, I thought. I raced to the bedroom window; I peered in. Blue flames surrounded the bed, which was in shambles. I couldn't see anyone. I hurried to the kitchen window, but the window was too high and I darted to the next one--the utility room. I could see a washing machine, basin, and cleaning equipment. The door was slightly ajar. A woman lightly clad in summer clothing stood in the dimly lit room. I could see her arms and face had ruptured blisters from the blast burns. The searing heat had scorched her blouse and melted the plastic buttons. The locked window frames had been blown out, but there wasn't enough room for her to get out. To my amazement the woman just stood in the utility room doorway like a statue. She showed no visible signs of pain. She was bewildered and speechless. I called and beckoned her to the window. The woman neither heard nor saw me. I ran to a picket fence around the house and kicked a 4 x 4 post from the rotted gate and smashed a larger opening in the framed window. She began to move in painfully slow steps toward the opening. I finally reached for her at the waist and pulled her though the window. Thin layers of ruptured skin scraped off as pieces of glass from the broken window frame tore through her already mutilated body. I laid her on the grass and covered her with a white sheet which I had taken from the clothes line. She looked at me blankly; she said nothing. She couldn't answer any of my questions. In retrospect she must have been in deep shock.

I couldn't see but I could hear the blaring sirens of the police and ambulance cars as they approached the scene. The neighbors gathered on their doorsteps. A compassionate gentleman whose name I didn't know greeted me and helped me attend the victim. Struggling with my protective instincts, I allowed the gentleman to take over while I made sure the police and ambulance personnel attended to the woman. The unknown victim was whisked away in an ambulance and taken to the Coronado hospital. I quietly and quickly faded into the crowd and continued to make my way to the theater.

I couldn't squash my thoughts of the disaster, and I missed the most romantic sequences of Dorothy Lamour in a sarong. After the show I made my way back to the scene of the fire. Little did I know in the coming days I would witness many scenes like the one I looked upon; walls charred and blackened, shredded curtains dangling curiously through burned window frames, scorched shrubbery, shards of glass littering the streets. And finally I caught the smell of smoke and burned upholstery, wood, and what else had been trapped in the blast. This was one small incident in a neighborhood. Soon I learned that an entire continent could be defaced, that war marred all in its path-- nothing was untouchable or sacred in combat.

Still haunted by this incident 50 years later, I began digging through old newspapers and finally found the details of this tragedy. The article in the *Coronado Journal* read:

> Suicide Attempt Proves Fatal to Coronado Woman
> Mrs. Eva Armstrong, 44, of 901 Ninth street, died of burns and delayed shock Monday morning at 11:15 A.M. at the local hospital. Mrs. Armstrong had attempted suicide in her home early Sunday evening when she closed the windows and doors of her bedroom and opened the gas jets.
>
> Apparently impatient at the slow approach of death by asphyxiation, Mrs Armstrong struck a match, causing an explosion which was heard for many blocks.

The small cottage, owned by Harry O. Temple, formerly of Coronado was almost totally wrecked by the force of the explosion. The roof was blown off, all windows were blown out leaving the inside of the house in shambles. A minor fire was started by the explosion which was quickly extinguished by the fire department.

Two suicide notes were found, written to Charles R. Armstrong, husband of the deceased, who could give no motive for his wife's suicide. The body was sent to Benbough's Mortuary from where services were held yesterday.[1]

---

[1] Suicide Attempt Proves to Coronado Woman, Coronado Journal, November 19, 1942.

Thomas M. Rice

Ready for daily cycling, 1998, San Diego, CA

Trial by Combat

Thomas M. Rice, age 63, 10 K run, Coronado, CA, 3rd place

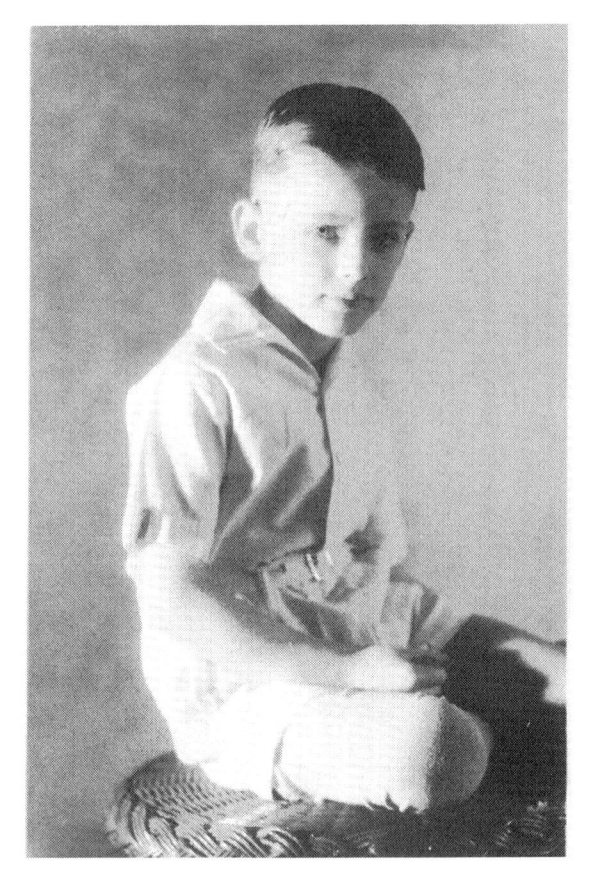

Thomas M. Rice

Thomas M. Rice, age 6yrs, Coronado, CA, circa 1927

Trial by Combat

Thomas M. Rice, pilot of Schweitzer sailplane, ready for take-off, Lake Elsinore, CA, 1987

TMR Officiating at Hilltop High School track meet, 1988, Chula Vista, CA

Chapter 3

Induction, Army Style

To lead untrained men into battle is to throw them away
                                        Confucius

Reliving the gruesome scene of the burned out house and the woman's charred body, I struggled to get some sleep that night. At 9:00 A.M., November 17, 1942, I and a dozen other civilian-recruits reported to the San Diego post office.

A young second lieutenant led the methodical swearing in ceremonies. We stood at attention around the United States flag embroidered with gold fringe. After we were sworn in and pledged to defend our great country, we were now considered to be the property of the United States Army. The Articles of War numbers 58 and 61 specifically bound us; these codes covered the crimes of desertion and absent without official leave (A.W.O.L.). With the first big step having been taken, we were excused and told to go home and put our lives in order, which sounded a bit ominous and terminal. Of course, for some it was. For others it was as long as the war or the army saw fit to keep us at their convenience.

The next day I reported to a sergeant at the post office. We boarded a bus and rode to Fort Rosecrans, San Diego. The second step in becoming a soldier was both humiliating and chaotic -- the physical examination. Army personnel had devised a process of room by room inspection of every inch of your body. It was bend over with the rubber glove treatment from behind: skin it down and pull it back. The procedure was termed "short arm inspection." This embarrassing exam made even the bravest soldier cringe with that primordial fear which haunts most men, the fear that their organ was smaller than it ought to be -- so use it or lose it but never abuse it, as Paul Fussell's thesis <u>Doing Battle</u> discussed.

As we gingerly walking to the next room a medic checked our eyes, ears nose and throat. We read an eye chart and took the Ishirhara color blind test. They asked us to cough and sneeze as they checked our throats and made sure that nothing was ruptured. Moving into another inspection area, a medic examined our feet for fallen arches and other deformities. We proceeded to have our lungs checked with some deep breathing and maximum volume. Our blood pressure registered must be within the normal range for our age, and finally a hearing test at maximum distance and lowest volume.

Each step was a series of mental jocular experiences, accompanied by formal written reports that would be presented to the next examiner all day long. The team of doctors and medics could inspect twenty-five recruits an hour. With our bodies thoroughly poked and prodded, we got dressed. The final terse warning yelled at us was, "Flies spread disease, keep yours buttoned!"

The organized army medical personnel kept all of our records in proper order as we hurried up and waited for most of the day, shifting from foot to foot. Our last medical treatment came rather quickly, with a series of inoculations on both arms at the same time and before you could look one way or the other, the job was done. Through all this we were never served a meal.

As night fell, a large group of us boarded a train, and were sent to Fort MacArthur in San Pedro, California. A group leader carried our induction papers. Upon arrival he surrendered these forms to the admitting non-commissioned officer. We were then shuffled off to a buffet dinner, army style of course. At 2:00 A.M. a cook slapped unrecognizable meat, vegetable and hot mashed potatoes on to our metal tray. Smiling, he then plopped a three flavored ice cream sandwich directly into the hot mashed potatoes ; we were all dismayed to say the least and watched it melt into spumoni.

Having eaten a hasty one-dish meal, they herded us into a large colorless room with a seating capacity of several thousand. It was getting late when we each sat at a desk where a pencil and folded test booklet lay. We waited for instructions. This was the mental examination; the army recorded the results which followed you throughout your entire military service. These specific tests were above the average high school level and included some interesting sections.

With the orders read, we placed headphones over our ears. A series of Morse code signals sounded. We were required to write down each "dot, dot and dash, dash" in the note book that represented a letter. I knew many of the coded signals but I suddenly realized that the Army was looking for communication men-- radio operators; I didn't want to be one. I attempted to mark all of the answers wrong in order to gain the desired results. When the results of the test were handed out, I quietly jumped for joy when I saw the word "disqualified."

The next two days I remained at Fort MacArthur. Here the new recruits with oversized and undersized bodies received their undersized and oversized uniforms. Pre war enlistees, early 1941, had been issued white accessories: boxed type underwear, socks, t-shirts, white towels, etc. This led us to believe that we would be treated as civilized people. By 1942, however, new experiments in camouflage dictated that everything, underwear and toiletries, handkerchiefs, pipe cleaners (who in the hell uses these?), and toilet paper were to be issued in olive -drab. We looked like an enormous sea of green bustling about in our funny uniforms.

After we donned our new attire, haircuts were ordered. All of the naive recruits asked the barber to, "save a little on the sides and the top, please." That request fell upon dead ears as the barber spun the chair in place and started the shaver 'humming.' Every bit of hair was on the floor! Protesting brought trouble as most of us swallowed our pride; this was the Army's way to cut hair! With shaven heads we were then issued our army serial numbers (ASN) - otherwise known as dog tags because the military unceremoniously referred to us as dogs or dog faces. To drive this home we ate in a mess hall and were fed K rations or canine food, and issued shelter - half pup tents. Our dog tags included two metal plates, each 1" x 2." We wore those on a chain around our necks like a collar. You don't take the dog tags off. Inscribed in small letters was your name, army serial number, parents name and address, blood type and religious preference were required to memorize our ASN backwards and forwards.

Another dehumanizing term introduced to us was GI. We were ' government issue' somewhat like shiny, galvanized garbage cans. GI simply stood for a soldier -- one with no human qualities, mass-produced, a faceless creature, like a bottle on an assembly line. All the same color, same shape, and same content with the same label. They addressed us as "private" even though there was nothing private about the army. We served at the government, s convenience.

To beat into us that we weren't in a civilized atmosphere anymore, a new language of anomalies was thrown at us. I won't repeat most of them, but army verbiage led to the sociology of the obscene. The language made reference to the major erogenous zones, portions of the human anatomy that didn't differentiate between male and female, and a rich assortment of alementary expressions of the eliminatory functions. It was my experience that no one hid their shock at the constant use of the obscenities used by the noncoms. Surprisingly, I didn't remember hearing an officer using any profanity in our presence. Possibly this meant that the officers realized that a leader could lose respect if they used a plethora of curse words or maybe I was just becaming numb to the use of vulgar language.

In just three days of indoctrination I had been humiliated both physically and emotionally; I had learned many curse words and new expressions, and had been introduced to an olive drab world. It was an ugly dimension in which I found myself and yet my drive to compete and get those wings allowed me to stay. After our induction they separated eight of us from the group. I was put in charge of our records, and we boarded a train. Southern Pacific Railroad transported us across the continent to Camp Toccoa, Georgia, a basic paratroop training camp. The trip across country took a toll on all eight of us. We were all jammed into one compartment -- no

Trial by Combat

private baths--the tight setting triggered several fistfights. One bully insisted we open the records for fun. We could read our scenarios aloud and laugh our heads off. I refused to open any of the records. If we had arrived at Camp Toccoa with even one opened we would all have been sent to a "straight leg outfit" (regular army infantry unit). I wasn't going to risk losing my pair of paratroopers wings just for some cheap laughs. Sure enough the bully didn't like my tone of voice, and he took a swipe at me. A brief brawl ensued, those records remained closed!

Bruised and battered, we arrived at the train station near Camp Toccoa four days after leaving California. It was late afternoon of November 27, 1942, a crisp, damp Thanksgiving Day.

After disembarking from the train we jumped aboard a truck which transported us to Camp Toccoa. The truck bumped along the Georgia road ; the fall air was crisp as I filled my lungs with good clean country air. Camp Toccoa lay near Highway 13 and comprised about 17, 000 acres of rough mountain terrain in the northeast corner of Georgia. One mile adjacent to the camp Mount Currahee loomed; it would soon become a curse word to all of us.

Toccoa had been previously referred to as Camp Toombs, named after Brigadier General Robert Toombs, a fiery and fierce Confederate commander during the American Civil War. Ironically, an old abandoned casket factory building was situated near the site.

Military personnel escorted us to a tented area called "Company W" on the perimeter of the camp, isolated from the 506 th Parachute Infantry Regiment which was at the end of their basic training. With the ranks of this unit filled, another parachute regiment was needed. The recruits assembled in Company W which would make up this unit - 501st Parachute Infantry Regiment.

I lay in my tent thinking about the impending weeks. We were here to be physically hardened and to be mentally molded so that we could withstand any battle scenario. Could I complete even the 13 weeks of basic training, in a camp set up to be conducted during the late winter and early spring? Could I complete the exercises with extreme sleep, food and water deprivation? I couldn't honestly answer these questions, but I knew one thing, I was here to beat anything the army threw at me. I wanted those wings!

We rose early the next morning and marched to the crudely made thirty- four foot high aircraft fuselage mounted on stilts. The only way in was by a ladder, the only exit was via a parachute. This was our first airborne test. It was "show your guts now or get out." A cadre segreant roughly attached each of us, one at a time to a parachute harness. The harness was connected to a pulley and anchored to a 200 yard steel cable that ran along the fuselage to a saw dust pit. A brawny sergeant yelled out brief instructions: "Each of you will take a turn jumping from this tower, make a quarter turn to your left; keep your chin to your chest or you'll get knocked out; keep your legs together: arms crossed at chest level; elbows tucked in; you will count out loud' one thousand, two thousand, three thousand ' and you will land safely in the sawdust pit below."

Easy for him to say! I stepped up to the doorway, closed my eyes and made that leap of faith. As I counted--one thousand, two thousand, three thousand--I felt my stomach lurch, struggling to break free from my body. Many times I had experienced nightmares of falling and often jerked myself awake from that awkward feeling of plunging into a blackened abyss. Maybe this was all a bad dream. I could imagine the local newspaper headlines." Another wannabe paratrooper dies while trying to be a man. Just about then the guide wire caught; it bounced me up and down only a few feet from the ground. I safely sailed down into the sawdust pit like a Hail Mary touchdown pass. I was alive and my terror had been contained! Our bully friend from the train lost his wits at the mock-up tower ;we never saw him again.

Thinking I had passed and could join the 501st Parachute Infantry Regiment (PIR), I was surprised when an officer ordered me to report to the commanding officer of the 501st, Colonel Howard R. Johnson. The colonel interviewed each of us. He was looking for aggressive, athletic and competitive soldiers. Colonel Johnson didn't want to waste time trying to manufacture a pugnacious spirit; he was looking for natural fighters. My high school and college athletic records satisfied the colonel; round two was over. We moved on to the regimental psychologist. The shrink sorted out the

Trial by Combat

trouble-makers and malcontents. The saying in those days was: If you could hear lightning and see thunder, you couldn't get in the `army. If you could see lightning and hear thunder you could get in the army. If you were thunder and you were lightening you could get in the airborne!

I still marvel and am facinated by this trial of terror because it came so early in my army airborne military service- November 28, 1942. as an obstacle to airborne regiments- a unique challenge.

The spark that ignited the burning desire to develop a low altitude terrorizing apparatus as a jump qualification for airborne battalions and regiments was the necessity to save time in training, to save money, to save effort and to eliminate the faint-hearted soldier. This apparatus made complete the four stages of airborne training.

Those of us who made it through the three trials were barracked in a tent dubbed "Casual Company." Here we waited to be assigned to a company, platoon, and squad. I was ordered to report to C Company, third platoon.

The officer corps of the 501st PIR was made up of West Point graduates; an experienced cadre of platoon sergeants from the old army formed the non-commissioned officers (NCOs).

The rest of us were ranked as privates, which is no rank at all. We all faced the unseeing challenges--how to stay in the airborne for the next 13 weeks. This was going to be the second phase of the weeding-out process. The fear of failing was ever present and hung over all of us. As I looked around the barracks, I could see several recruits weaker, skinnier and dumber than me. Confidence puffed me up. I could see the stars. We were an endangered species for the thunder and lightning never ceased. I can still hear the rolling thunder. I felt as though I had only taken the first step on a long and dangerous journey--the journey to becoming an airborne soldier. I dreaded most of the ordeal that lay ahead, but there were several things I was looking forward to. I had always liked meeting a challenge, and this was certainly going to be challenging. The other thing was that I was very impressed with the caliber of the officers who would be leading us especially Colonel Howard R. Johnson.

Chapter 4

Basic Training
Knocking the Civilian Out of Us

*An army without discipline is no more than a mob,
alternating between frightened sheep and beasts of prey.*
                              Field Marshal Sir William J. Slim

Airborne Command Number 4, initiated November 4, 1942, stated that airborne troops would undergo 37 week of training. The training would be divided into three phases, Phase 1 include 13 weeks of individual basic training.[1] From November 1942 to March 1943 the 501st PIR scratched and plowed its way through 13 weeks of brutal physical and mental exercises. Officers tried to teach us pissed-off newcomers the art of military order and discipline. They were trying "to knock the civilians out of us."

Ordinary soldiers defended themselves from the grossest kind of chicken shit by devising humor, rumor, jokes, and finally maneuvering outside of the of the bonds and bounds of military convention.

---
[1] Airborne Command Number 4, initiated November 4, 1942, stated that airborne troops would undergo 37 weeks of training. The training would be divided into three phases. Phase 1 included 13 weeks of individual basic training. Rapport and Northwood, <u>Rendezvous With Destiny,</u> pge. 26.

29

In that time the army hoped to achieve several goals: 1) make us physically fit so that our bodies could withstand the future torture that we would be put through--physical training (PT) as we called it, 2) introduce us to an assortment of weapons and their tactical usage, 3) the military hoped to sever us from civilian life. Farewell to privacy, farewell to my civilian clothes. In supreme display of my patronage, I threw my civilians clothes in a GI trash can. I was in the army now! I will never forget the aroma of Camp Toccoa in the winter of 1942. The smell unfamiliar to me of anthracite coal smoke, the tediousness of ten hours of training, the ever present communicable diseases, and the sectional diffusion of language.

Colonel Johnson and his officers were faced with the task of transforming hordes of military sows' ears into silk purses. They had to manage a wide range of recalcitrant youths as recruits: clod busters, fruit pickers, cattle pushers, snake charmers, welfare recipients, calamity howlers, whispering mongers, gold brickers, malcontents, jail birds, all anxious to cast off their shackles. Some were insects that metamorphoses into doing things that have meaning and purpose--intellectual snobs, of which I was one. Some had soft hands and weak-kneed scholars. These were the ones that sat most of the day pondering an academic assignment. All airborne boys, later men, were driven by a strong sense of curiosity for adventure, admiration, glory and recognition. Beneath all of this was a sense of connection to God for some meaning, for some purpose, a realization rightfully understood. Some found injury, some found death. The officers' first method of handling us crumbs was to break us down into smaller units, get some order out of chaos. A officer assigned me to Company C, third platoon, third squad. Company C was 128 strong; we belonged to the 1st Battalion of the 501 PIR. Our company commander was Captain Robert Phillips. How the officers decided who was detailed to which unit was beyond the rank and file's knowledge, but we didn't lose any sleep over this mystery. We just thought it was an intriguing puzzle.

Our days began at the crack of dawn; I could smell the scent of anthracite coal smoke which permeated the icy mornings. We would fall out, in formation, in the company street to begin a new 10 hours of training. During one early morning PT (physical training) exercise Colonel Johnson appeared unannounced. We were running piggy back relay races. The colonel looked at me, jumped on my back and said, "Let's go!" I ran 200 yards at full speed. I was terrified that I wouldn't live up to his standards, or would drop the Colonel. I feared he was testing the physical conditioning of the first battalion and company C was being put on the spot.

At the turn around point, Colonel Johnson jumped off my back and beckoned me to get on board. At my 137 pounds Colonel Johnson had it much easier than I did carrying his 150 pounds. Evidentially he was satisfied with our conditioning because he smiled as he passed Captain Phillips in a springy quick step and said nothing, and disappeared.

An Ideology Created An Idol
Colonel Howard R. Johnson

Colonel Johnson was one of a kind, a singular personality.

He was born in Maryland, June 23, 1903. He had light brown hair, leathery sunburnt skin, extraordinary piercing eyes and slender frame. As a young man he excelled in athletics. He was a four letter man at Central High School, Washington, D.C. He entered the Naval Academy in 1923. After two years he left the academy to join the Army Air Corps, but was rejected due to his insufficient side vision. He returned to the army and reinvented the Queen of Battles-the infantry.

In subsequent years he attended various army schools, after which he grew tired and bored with post-war depression military exercises with broom sticks for guns, make-believe field operations and garrison life. He longed for daily action challenges.

Still disillusioned with army war games, maneuvers, and looking for new challenges, he discovered that a new experiment in airborne regiments was being organized. He jumped at the chance to command, even though he wasn't enamoured by parachuting.

In the early 1940's, he flipped over a jeep, crushing several spinal veterbrea, which almost ended his military career. He was left with a slight forward hunch.

In November, 1942, Colonel Johnson and his cadre of regimental officers, Lieutenant Ed Jansen, C Company, being one of them, formed the 501st Parachute Infantry Regiment at Camp Toombs, Georgia.[2]

Knowing we had pleased our regimental commander made us proud; our morale rose for a few days but it didn't last. We learned very early at this stage of the game we were considered 99% infantry and 1% paratroopers. Like the millions of foot soldiers, who had gone down the road of military history, we endured a lot of walking and running exercises. Over the next 13 weeks, I had to make a continuous 25 -mile march in 8 hours, a 9-mile trek in two hours--weighted down with full field equipment and only one canteen of water, which was not to be opened unless an officer gave you direct orders to drink. This activity was termed "water discipline." It felt more like torture than discipline. At times we wondered who the enemy was.- Our officers were likely suspects; there weren't any Germans around. Besides the 25 and the 9 mile hikes we accomplished a 5 mile excursion in one hour. We wore out the soles of our shoes at an accelerated speed.

If someone in formation couldn't keep up with the pace- setters, that individual had to run with his hands over his head. While trouncing around we had to yell cadence. It was the language of obscenity again and again most of which are too vulgar to repeat. The more notable one goes like this:

> This my rifle, this is my gun
> {the soldier places one hand over his crotch}.
> One is for fighting, one is for fun.

In retrospect they were horrible, ugly little not so nursery rhymes. The cadence was just a small tactic to pull us away from our comfortable civilian lives.

We accomplished all of this through extremely unpleasant daily icy weather, something I wasn't used to in Southern California. Soon company C's morning sick call list grew. Battalion doctors

---

2 Sampson, Francis, <u>Look out Below</u>, pge.21.

were notified that something was afoot. Sure enough third platoon was suffering from an outbreak of measles. The medical authorities isolated all thirty-six soldiers from the organized company activities and quarantined us to our Quonset huts during the evening hours.. The third platoon conducted all of its training apart from the other two platoons, and we weren't allowed any recreational time with them.

It didn't take long before we grew restless; we had Quonset hut fever. I volunteered to break quarantine and sneak over to the post exchange and buy the 3rd platoon a carton of Milky Way candy bars. This was my first covert, military maneuver in the face of the adversary. I nonchalantly walked over to the PX when I knew it would be crowded, hoping I would blend in and go unnoticed. The expedition was successfully completed in quick time; we all savored our booty. The next day 1st Sergeant Marshal Buckridge arrived at our hut and told me Captain Phillips wanted to see me. 1st Sergeant Buckridge escorted me to the orderly room and then into the captain's office. I stood at attention in the captain's growling presence. He informed me that I had been spotted in the post exchange store. Captain did all the talking as he interrogated me, and he expected the truth. My answer to all of his questions was "Yes sir. No excuse sir. My fault, Sir!" I figured he already knew anyway, there didn't seem to be any sport in trying to lie. I was admonished and I had to face the consequences. The captain seemed satisfied with my candor. Now came the sentencing. Captain Phillips assigned me to what he thought was a stiff and grueling punishment. I was to run up Mount Currahee; this meant I was to go it alone and return non-stop. The mountain rose to a thousand feet at a steep angle most of the way. A round trip was a distance of seven miles.

This was like throwing a rabbit in a briar patch. The captain had no idea of my high school and college track and cross - country achievements. Saluting Captain Phillips, I left, I wasn't going to argue. Captain Phillips felt I was too relaxed about my run, and just to make sure I obeyed his order, he drove a jeep alone to the top of the mountain. Phillips parked the vehicle behind several large boulders and waited to see if I would carry out his command.

As I topped the summit and turned to descend I caught a glimpse of the company commander in this jeep. I gave no sign of recognition but continued down the mountain. Returning to barracks I showered. A sergeant arrived at my hut and informed me the captain wanted to see me in his office again-- twice in one day! It felt like *de ja vu*. Phillips grilled me with a plethora of questions. He couldn't understand how I had made the run so fast without cheating somehow. I made no mention of seeing him in the jeep. Captain Phillips' demeanor changed, and he told me that he had lived in San Diego when he was a kid. Beneath it all, it appeared the commander was testing me. He was looking for some semblance of leadership qualities. Phillips needed reliable soldiers in combat. I had respected his order and successfully carried it out, even though it was a little excessive. The mountain was steep and dangerous in the twilight on the trail.

After our brief discussion, Captain Phillips summarily dismissed me and I returned to the hut. Quarantine was soon lifted; two weeks had gone by. We struggled hard to play catch - up with the other two platoons. A few days had passed since I had been freed when I was again called, a third time, to Captain Phillips' office. "What had I done this time?" I thought to myself. A second lieutenant led me to an S-2 command car. The vehicle stopped just outside the company grounds. The lieutenant briefed me on the art and methods of gathering intelligence information. The lieutenant directed me to watch the regimental mental area-specifically, I was to keep alert to anyone photographing the equipment: the new paratroop gear, folding stock carbines, bazookas, shape charges and gas masks. Even though most of these items were not in general use and many hadn't been unveiled, it was feared there were spies among us. There was concern over pacifist and non-compliance groups. Two were in our area: one at the Union Theological Seminary and a group of Seminole Indians who boycotted military service and retreated into the Florida Everglades.

The lieutenant directed me to give weekly reports via letter. I was to provide detailed account of what I observed throughout the camp grounds. The letter was mailed and addressed to the local post office at Southern Pines. Lt. Sims, regimental S-2, assigned me a code

Trial by Combat

name, "Elmer" and furnished me with embossed paper, envelopes, stamps and the address. He cautioned me to be observant.

When I wasn't conducting my clandestine projects or PT exercises, the officers began introducing us to an assortment of weapons and assimilating combat scenarios into our daily routine. We learned to load and fire the carbine, Garand M1 rifle and the Thompson sub-machine gun, and to throw an assortment of hand grenades; they taught us how to field strip our weapons and then reassemble the mixed parts, blindfolded, within minutes. We then moved out to the rifle range for practice after zeroing in the rifle. The target was at a distance of 200 yards.

They trained us to focus on intensification of fire power - not accuracy. We took a crack at firing the Browning machine gun (BAR) out on the rifle range. We were to move the machine gun fire horizontally and vertically while firing and attempt to put three bullets in a two inch square on the diagonal; spraying the mark with holes and thus getting good coverage on the target. I placed all of my shots in the wooden framework and was subsequently disqualified as a machine gunner.

From this machine gun drill and other firing exercises we determined that they weren't training us to be marksmen. Precision shooting wasn't going to win the war. The only way to do it was by sprinting toward the enemy and firing from the hip. We called it assault fire or fire and movement and learned to throw ourselves into combat. Rush the enemy and don't give him a chance to recover. Saturate the area with bullets, pour it on in the general direction of the enemy. It was a matter of simple deduction. If you have three enemy soldiers manning a machine gun, you throw five hand grenades and blast the area with counter rifle and machine gun fire. A projectile would certainly hit one adversaries if not three, or at least chase them the hell away from your position. It is a frightening feeling for the enemy to see bullets from rifles and machine guns blasting all around him while you scream for aggressive charging. My weapon was a Thompson .45 caliber sub-machine gun. It was hand tooled, and at close range, accurate and deadly, but beyond fifty yards, it was ineffective. The Army eventually replaced the Thompson sub-machine gun with the grease gun, an undependable steel fabrication.

After spending many hours on the rifle range, we moved to the battlefield obstacle course, a maze of barbed wire zig-zagged everywhere, 18 inches above our head. We crawled on our hands and knees with our weapon in the bow of our elbows. To simulate realism the cadre placed animal intestines and other innards on the crawling path and shot over our heads with rapid machine gun fire. TNT periodically exploded close by. We sweated through this in a day and made a couple of night maneuvers.

Once we made it past the obstacle course and learned to fire our weapons, the officers attempted to demonstrate to us pissed - off recruits hand - to- hand combat, knife fighting and judo. There were plenty of black eyes, bruises, cuts and even some broken bones to keep the camp hospital corps busy.

By the twelfth week of basic training we were all anxious to move on to the second phase of training. When the officers informed us that we were going airborne we cheered because we didn't know any better. Naively, we thought the hiking and marching was over. Turned out we weren't leaving right away, and the captain organized a little running event for us. Here we go running up this damn mountain again on a Sunday. I wound up racing one of my buddies, Guy Sessions. He thought he could beat me, but I stepped up the pace and came in first, he was a close second. Major Julian Ewell, Regimental Headquarters, came in third. We didn't even recognize him at first and began patting him on the back for coming in a distant third. I think Sessions and I spotted the gold leaf on his fatigues at the same time; Major Ewell wasn't smiling. We abruptly stopped patting his shoulder. I couldn't figure how I hadn't noticed him. I was always careful to hold back so as not to embarrass any of the officers. Out doing an officer in a running event was like breaking quarantine. I didn't want to run Mount Currahee twice in the same day, but thankfully, no negative consequences arose from us beating Major Ewell in the race. We faded into the platoon once the rest of the men finished the event.

Orders finally came down from regimental headquarters to move out. We had finished basic training at Camp Toccoa. We were heading to Fort Benning, Georgia. Phase 2 of our airborne training was about to begin. I wasn't quite clear what Phase 1 had really taught me. For the past 13 weeks we had endured repetitive, rough, taxing and unrelenting training and a lot of military lore. It had been like going back to school: chanting songs, school colors, and adapting to a strict order of all things, some foolish. But unlike civilian schools we learned civility here. We were taught to destroy and survive in a dimension that didn't take prisoners and the ultimate consequences were life or death. In retrospect, I think its aim was not to prepare us for battle but to make us long for it, and to harass the men in time of peace, in such a way that they look upon it with glee, during the time of war

HELL ON CURAHHEE

ON COMMAND
THE SOUND OF POUNDING FEET MEN
RUNNING UP THE STEEP

FULL GEAR PUFFING AND WHEEZING
MUSCLES STRAINING TO THE EXTREME
ONWARD TO THE TOP
SEVEN MILES WITHOUT A STOP

THE AGONY, WHOSE IDEA
HIDDEN FAR FROM ENEMY EYES
THEY TRAIN FOR HITLER'S HELL
WHEN WILL IT END

NEED EVERY BIT TO BEAT HITLER'S BAND UP
THE MOUNTAIN CRACK OF DAWN IN THROUGH
THE FOG IN EARLY MORN

HERE AIRBORNE MEN ARE BEING BORN
BY THE SPIRIT OF BILL LEE
ON THE SLOPES OF CURAHHEE
WHICH MEANS "STAND ALONE"
                                    Anonymous

Chapter 5

Fort Benning - Jump School

If a man has a tent of linen, with all of the openings sealed up, he will be able to throw himself from a great height without injury.

                              Benjamin Franklin

    Fort Benning lies astride the Chatahoochie River, the ox bow boundary between Georgia and Alabama. It was and still is the center of airborne facilities to train infantrymen and armored divisions.[1]

    The magnet of parachuting began to pull boys and men from organized National Guard units, draftees and volunteers from around the United States, in a rush. They came battalion by battalion and met another magnet that could or would pull them to their death in ten seconds if the parachute did not open.

    They all knew that they would be ordered to stand up, jump, and face a determined enemy, who wanted to kill them. No other generation of young American men before had to consider this

---

[1] Fort Benning lies astride the Chattahoochie River, which is the natural oxbow boundary between Georgia and Alabama. There was and still is the center of airborne facilities to train infantrymen into airborne regiments. Critchell, <u>Four Stars of Hell, </u>p.8.

possibility in military service. The sense of purposeful excitement was felt from the jump towers to the latrines, from the parade grounds to the parachute packing sheds, from the C-47's to the jump master's commands.[2]

So it was, that Fort Benning was flooded with new volunteers eager to try jumping from airplanes. Those who languished in military jails were eager to shed their irons and the army was eager to have them in an emergency. Those in the military stockades could be assured of their release if they signed up for the airborne. In some cases, those already in civilian slammers would be left off the hook if they enlisted in the paratroops. This practice continued until after the Korean war[3]

Men in the stockades were up at 4:00 A.M. marching to K.P. with a white band buttoned to their upper sleeve or a large white "P" painted on the back of their blue jacket, followed by an M.P. at eight paces carrying a loaded shot gun at high port arms.

If anything was possible at Camp Toccoa, Fort Benning was impossible, being more miserable than Camp Toccoa. All airborne troops were quartered in the notorious "frying pan " area. It was an infamous city of tar paper shanties and tents, row upon row, just above Lawson Field, anchored on sandy soil, barren of trees but not of heat. This is where the 501st Parachute regiment learned that during jump training we were not permitted to walk-only double time nor were we allowed to lean against anything or have our hands in our pockets.[4] This is where the cadre commanded jump training grates and bruises your hide every day all day for four weeks.

The Rubicon for most airborne trainees, then (1942) and now was the one thirty-four foot "mock-up" jump tower at Camp Toccoa and the six thirty-four foot towers at Fort Benning. If a man is afraid of heights and falling in space, then he will quit here, more than the imposing two-hundred fifty foot towers, from which the jumper

---

[2] Battalion by battalion men and boys rushed to the fort (Benning). It was the magnet of parachuting that they sensed as a powerful excitement that could pull them to their death in ten seconds. Orflea, Lost Battalion, p.29.
[3] The practice continued until the end of the Korean War. Ibid, p.30.
[4] We weren't allowed to lean against anything, stand straight erect nor were we ever to be seen with our hands in our pockets, Sampson, Francis, Look out Below, pge 8.

Trial by Combat

doesn't get a real sense of the ground. The thirty-four foot tower is considered a psychological barrier, for the ground is too visible from which to recover and you could see a worm crawling.[5] This is where the worm turns.

Fort Benning Parachute School training was conducted in four stages: A, B, C, D, each lasting one week. It was ironic that our jump zones in the Normandy invasion were designated A, B, C, D. The 501st Parachute Infantry Regiment skipped stage A, to the dismay of the cadre because of our excellent physical condition and the compression of time that was allotted to qualify the graduates to jump status.

Stage B was four hours of physical training and four hours of parachute nomenclature and parachute harness indoctrination; how to collapse a parachute and how to exit from and airplane in flight. At the parade ground physical training site, upon our arrival, the NCO's(noncommissioned officers in charge of the cadre) took command. The biggest and toughest "bronzed Apollo" was known as "Flash Gordon." His undershirt stretched his biceps to infinity and his jump boots were polished to piano luster. All of the cadre used jump school jargon, much of which we had never heard before, but we got used to it as time went on. If you did not execute a cadre order in snap order, you would hear this dirty little ditty, loud and clear,

> Your soul belongs to God,
> But your ass belongs to me.

We gave the remaining cadre nicknames, none of which were complimentary, even embarrassing in army language. I remember "bracing" standing at attention with my eyes riveted straight ahead, neck muscles tight as possible, veins bulging and counting the almost invisible hairs on the front of the sergeants head and yelling like you had a pair of buffalo balls,

"Sir! My serial number is 19164859, Sir!!!"

---

5 The thirty-four foot tower is considered a psychological barrier, for the ground is too visible for which to recover. Orfalea, Lost Battalion, pge. 39-40.

The next step in Stage B was to gain some experience on the wind machine. The purpose was to learn how to collapse a parachute under windy landing conditions. I was given a parachute harness without the parachute attached. I was directed to lie on the ground in front of the wind machine while a cadre attached a parachute. The high velocity wind generated by the wind machine dragged me across the ground on my back. The procedure was to grab the left two risers or the right two risers, pull the knees up to the chest and execute a fast front flip onto the feet and run parallel to the axis of the wind and collapse the parachute by reeling in the appropriate risers until the parachute deflates.

The during the week we did fuselage mock-up tower jumps from the thirty-four foot tower and parachute landing falls in all directions. The parachute landing falls were done from a six foot platform and from a three foot diameter ring as it slids down an incline cable. The NCO would release the suspended paratrooper unannounced and call for a left or right landing to be executed in perfect form. The punishment was fifty push-ups for failure. These exercises were the essence for a safe landing. Many officers could not take this kind of overseeing by lower rank tutors and dropped out.

Stage C consisted of the proper procedures and safety in the aircraft, four hours of physical close combat training and packing the main parachute for five qualifying jumps. The parachute packing was done on long smooth packing tables at Lawson Field. The main parachute back pack was opened on each table and we were instructed about the number and make-up of the parachute panels, suspension lines, risers, break cord, apex vent collar and the 'D' ring. A team of two paratroopers worked through the entire process, each checking the other for exactness. We were issued a booklet for detailed study. The last day of the week Friday, I packed my parachute for the first qualifying jump Monday. The parachute I packed was the one that I would use to jump. There were many checks and counter-checks and the NCO's hovered over each team checking for details and proper procedures. When finished, I signed my name to the packing card and attached it to the backpack of the parachute.

Anxiety began to build over the week-end. We heard all sorts of gruesome stories about death and sanguine paratrooper songs such as "Blood on the Risers." Stage C was not without numerous heart-pounding experiences on the two-hundred foot static jump towers. William Ryder, commander of the original Test Platoon in 1940, asked for volunteers to do something new a fifty foot vertical free fall from the top of the two-hundred foot jump tower with face and belly down before the runner chord caught.[6] By 1942, each paratrooper was expected to experience this same fall. I would lie on the ground, face down, after donning a parachute harness which was hooked to a long steel cable and raised under one of the arms of two-hundred foot tower. At one hundred feet above the ground and on the command of the NCO, "Pull," I reached for the "D" ring and pulled hard, transferring it to the other hand. I would free fall fifty feet or more and bounce several times, then lowered to the ground. If I dropped the "D" ring I would be raised to the next height which would be another hundred feet and the process would be repeated. If I failed to pull the 'D' ring after the third command or dropped it, I would be washed out of the corps, returned to barracks and disappear.

In the last exciting exercise I was harnessed to a parachute with a canopy spread around the circumference of a thirty foot basket, raised to two-hundred fifty feet and automatically released, set free and floated to an approved landing without getting entangled in the tower. If the wind was blowing hard an NCO would guide the jumper.

Stage D. A new week will start today, Monday, and progress through to Friday with exactness and in trepidation to graduation ceremonies on Saturday, the awarding of the coveted silver paratrooper wings. We came here not for feathers but for wings.

Airborne Command Order of November 4, 1942 states that each recruit shall make five parachute jumps at twelve hundred hundred feet, on command from a C-47 aircraft (DC-3) over the drop zone at Fort Benning, Georgia. I made one parachute jump each day and packed my parachute for the second jump the afternoon of the first day. Night jumps weren't required during the early developmental

---

6 Colonel Ryder was commander of the Test Platoon-1940. He asked for volunteers to try an experimental exercise. Ibid pge.40.

stages of parachuting. This would come later, as it did in England, during Operation Tiger.

The reveille whistle blew, and army songs blared at us over the public address system. Roll call was taken, and after breakfast the battalion assembled at the packing shed to view a horrifying sight. A C-47 droned over the drop zone at 1200 feet, and a jumper in characteristic form leaped from the aircraft and tumbled to the ground without an open parachute, trailing red smoke. We were dumbfounded by this accident and mortified by the horror of it. The word, very soon, was passed around that the jumper was a mannequin and this was the daily procedure to test the wind direction before the day of jumping began. The Airborne Command was testing us psychologically.

At the packing shed, we checked out our main and reserve parachutes and helped each other using the buddy system to don our equipment for the first jump. I put on my main back pack parachute by working each arm through the right and left harness straps and snapped a buckle to a chest level center ring. Two leg straps came between the legs and attached to two lower harness snap buckles, one on each leg. You had to bend slightly forward with the main parachute balanced on your back and with the knees slightly bent in order to tighten the leg straps. If you don't position the leg straps properly, right and left, the opening shock might render you sterile and distract you from a good landing, more like a raving maniac for several hours. If the riser buckle hit you on the head, the maniacal airborne dance could be much worse-riser burns. Upon landing, the drop zone safety airborne operations officer would fill the air with sulfuric epitaphs for your errors. Guts and glory! The first jump.

Quickly, we were prepped and inspected; it was hurry up and wait. We complained about our rigormortis stance until it was time to board the aircraft. Two sticks (a number of paratroopers) boarded, in reverse jumping order, as we were seated on opposite sides of the aircraft and strapped in. Without delay we were airborne amid engine roar, fuselage vibration, wind howling, and worst of all recruit silence. This was my first time in an aircraft with only one way out. We gained altitude to 1200 feet, crossed over the Chatahoochee River and banked into the drop zone pattern in Alabama.

Trial by Combat

The jump master gave a series of sharp verbal orders reinforced by physical signals, so that there would be no misunderstanding. We were going to jump about 4 seconds apart. A swat on the derriere was the 'go' signal, as you positioned yourself in the door. Four inches of the left boot extended outside the door, right foot back for balance, each hand slightly touching the side of the jump door, not gripping it, knees slightly bent for a spring forward and looking out, never down. It is the Army way. When the swat was delivered by the jump master, I either stepped out or swung my right leg out and made a quarter turn to the left, putting the prop blast behind me. The pilot throttled the aircraft to 105 knots air speed, with the tail high for a safe exit. Arms to be crossed over the reserve parachute, the legs to be held together with your chin pressed on your chest and counting aloud - one thousand, two thousand, three thousand, four thousand. ******* The counting, many jumps later, became a four letter word instead of "Geronimo."

Inside the aircraft, at 1200 feet, the jumping commands were:"stand up. At that instant, all jumpers stood up and made a quarter turn to the right to face the rear of the aircraft. I would be jumping number 4 in the first stick. The snapfastner was at the end of the static line and held in the left hand with the open part of the mechanism toward the anchor line cable. The anchor line cable ran the length of the fuselage and over the left shoulder. On command, "Hook up, " the open end of the snap fastener was anchored on the 2/3 inch diameter steel cable. I was now securely connected to the aircraft, as the snap fastener clicked into place. Upon hearing this characteristic sound, I was relieved. "Check your equipment." I tugged at all connecting links to make sure that they were secure. Then I checked the main back pack (parachute) of the jumper in front of me and made any adjustments to his webbing and static line to be sure that he was holding the snap fastener in the proper position. "Sound off for equipment check." From the last man in the stick, I heard "Nine ok, eight ok, seven ok, six ok, five ok, four ok," and so on. Finally, one ok. Number one 1 shouts, "All ok." The jump master goes to the end of the line and checks the last man, and returns to the door and shouts, "Are you ready?" The plane is filled with shouts of, "Let's get the hell out of here." The jump master shouted a new order, "Stand in the door." Everyone in the first stick shuffled forward, leading with the right foot, until we were compressed. The first jumper pivoted a quarter turn into the door and assumed the jumping stance. The jump master shouted, "Go" and swatted each jumper on the rear end, hard enough to garner his attention but not to distract him from the jump. The second jumper positioned himself in the door, in a like manner. The pilot had throttled the left engine back and we were cruising at 105 knots. The tail of the plane is lifted for a clean jump. This aircraft position is held until all jumpers are out and under a canopy. All jumpers are under their own canopies, free in the air, checking their position in relation to the other jumpers and the drop zone, especially the waiting ambulance with a big red cross on a field of white on the roof of the vehicle. The landing should be made with the knees slightly bent, dropped ankles and relaxed muscles for a parachute landing. All of these procedures were practiced hundreds of times which included physical training, tower drills, slip drills, wind machine and exit body positions, etc. All of these exercises were designed to keep us safe, if executed properly, over a five day exhibition jumping schedule. All of my jumps were uneventful except that I forgot numerous things thatIwas supposed to do, such as count and keep your eyes open.

After each parachute landing, I bagged my parachute, boarded a truck for a ride to the packing shed and lunch. I probably wouldn't get the same parachute I packed that afternoon.

Saturday morning, we sterilized the barracks above and beyond expectations and readied ourselves in 'class A' uniforms for graduation ceremonies. The acme of the ceremony was the pinning of the paratrooper's silver wings. In 1943, you had it pinned on by an officer, but twenty years later, the paratrooper had another choice, it was blood on the risers. The procedure was one which drew blood as a result of the wings being forced through your shirt and the prongs penetrating your flesh and made to bleed by hard pounding.This was done at your choice, penetration and pain without a grimace and a thank you sir. Hallelujah!!, Class number 64 had arrived with all privileges.

Trial by Combat

When we got back to the company area, each of us marched through the orderly room and were issued a month's pay plus jump pay of $50.00 and a ten day furlough with travel expenses paid.

Soldiers stationed at Fort Benning, Georgia, had a hand at the most celebrated good time home town in the country. The principle industry in Phenix City, Alabama, just across the state line from Fort Benning, Georgia, was sex, and its customer was the United States Army. The town was 80% devoted to the pillage of the airborne troops, called 'Uncle Sam's soldier boys. "There are only two things that a paratrooper liked to do more than drink beer. One was brawling, the other, slyly mentioned is sex, which was well-exercised while of leave with a few paratroopers screaming "Geronimo" on a two foot leap into a bed, 'B' girls, as they were called and hung out near Columbus, Alabama and other leave town as Atlanta, Georgia and New Orleans.Louisiana.[7]

The Southern Pacific railroad trip across the United States to San Diego from Fort Benning was uneventful , except that I gave my seat to a woman and I slept in the overhead baggage rack, in which I snugly fit. I arrived home in Coronado in a disheveled condition and discovered that only a few of my home town friends were still there. I felt disillusioned when I found the town shabbier and smaller. The others had shuffled off to military training camps throughout the United States. After a week of less than low grade excitement, I sought transportation back to the east coast. Herman Addelson, a 502nd paratrooper, who was on furlough in San Diego, was able to make arrangements for us to fly east in a Consolidated PBY aircraft as observers. Herman knew the daughter of the owner of Consolidated Aircraft Corporation, Major Ruben Fleet, and through her, he got us seats. Herman and I had been running on the Cross -Country team together at San Diego Sate College. The flight was from San Diego to Dallas, Texas, and an overnight stay. The next day we landed at Elizabeth City, North Carolina. I departed for Washington, D.C.after bidding farewell to Herman. This was the last time I would see my old college friend, or talk to him. He was killed in the early hours of D-Day when his aircraft, loaded with

---

7 There were many tales of paratroopers screaming "Geronimo" as they launched into a two foot leap into bed. Orfalea, Lost Battalion, pg41.

Thomas M. Rice

paratroopers, was shot up over the drop zone near Ste Mere Eglise, and it finally crashed in the English Channel.

On to Washington, D.C. to see a former girl friend, the daughter of an admiral. The evening was taken up at the Officer's Club, without a date, as a guest of the admiral. No dancing because all of the girls were with their favorite midshipmen in another room set aside for them. While everyone was dancing, I was alone at a table. A General, observing that I was an enlisted man in uniform and wearing jump boots, came to the table and engaged me in a warm conversation. He welcomed me. I told him how the airborne units were training and that I was having a good time, with tongue in cheek. The girls were still in the next room with their boy friends and in this instance, the general could do nothing for me other than issue me an invitation to join his party at an adjoining table. I courteously declined and he wished me god speed. I did not get a chance to dance all that evening. I never knew the name of the general. An enlisted man in an officer's club, what a demeaning situation, especially for the girls, to be dancing with a strange guest- an enlisted man.

As the years wore on to the fiftieth anniversary of the invasion of Europe, 1944, I met a number of admirals and generals who went out of their way to seek veterans who parachuted into Normandy, and gave them their fondest congratulations and a medal. They wished they could have been with us on D-Day, 1944, if you can believe that.

As the furlough wound down to the last few days I worked my way south from Chevy Chase, Maryland to Fort Benning, where the regiment was to reassemble and move to their new quarters at Camp MacKall, North Carolina. We had finished our jump training and were about to embark on a new and higher level of integrated and coordinated unit activity, which would ultimately test us in the Tennessee Maneuvers, as Blue Army aggressors. Before I arrived at Camp MacKall, I was assigned to a two week demolition course at Fort Benning, while the regiment relocated at Camp MacKall, North Carolina. The training dealt with the handling of British and American explosives of the latest design, such as T.N.T., British gun cotton, Nitrostarch, Composition C and Primachord.

With these components, we designed booby traps and all sorts of explosive devices of an incendiary nature. The final examination was a parachute jump from 700 feet with 12 fulminated mercury blasting caps, which were very dangerous if not padded and handled carefully.

A tragic accident occurred several days before the jump. A cadre sergeant was demonstrating the set-up of his own designed booby trap with a hidden trip wire. The explosive was a 1/2 pound of T.N.T. placed in the crotch of a tree. He had not yet secured it tightly in place. The explosive charge began to slip from the unsecured spot as the sergeant backed away. He reached for the charge before it could touch the ground and in doing so, he stepped on the hidden trip wire. The explosion took place, blew the tree crotch in shambles and severed his outreached right hand below the wrist. He was as brave a soul as I have ever seen, based on future experiences. He walked over to the command car with his arm over his head and had a tourniquet applied and tightened, as we stood frozen in intellect, and he was taken to the base hospital. The class was canceled for the day but the jump would take place on the following day. Watching a brave man getting his hand blown off was a brutal reminder to us all of what we had often been told: "There is no margin of error in training for the Airborne." The next step was that training would take place at Camp MacKall, and we knew at that facility things would be even more challenging and dangerous than anything we had experienced so far.

Chapter 6

Camp Mackall-Advanced Training

We all have a list of minuscule 'hells' in our heart and soul that is equal to the number of hairs on our head.

The 501 Parachute Infantry Regiment was at Camp MacKall, North Carolina, July, 1943 and training resumed at a higher level and a faster pace, with live ammunition exercises. It was company and battalion maneuvers with night exercises. Evidently we were supposed to like night fighting. The Germans said we hated night fighting, because they feared it most. Camp MacKall activities seemed to be a blur because the training was so repetitious, with longer hikes with full combat load in dusty summer weather, with fewer rest periods and a water quarantine on all 25 mile hikes.

On one 25 mile hike, under tactical conditions, my worn green fatigue uniform, called a jump suit, thread bare as it was, began to tear at the left knee. After many miles of annoying flapping; the tear circumnavigated the leg. I could stand it no longer and tore the pant leg off, at the next rest stop. I put the severed pant leg in my pocket. I looked rather odd with one pant leg on and the other off, a rag bag tail sergeant After we arrived at camp, I reported to the First Sergeant to explain my dilemma, showing him the tattered leg remnant. Before I had finished my display, he was yelling at me. His voice was like a rumbling volcano spewing pyrotechnics through his mahogany stained sugar pine tree face, to get that pant leg sewn on the jump suit and report to him. I mumbled inaudibly and politely under my breath, "Tojo eats worms." My head was clogged with anxiety from great resistance. This needle and thread surgery took about an hour. After the First Sergeant's inspection, declaring the work unacceptable and hopeless, he sent me to the Supply Sergeant, an old timer named Sgt. Huttner, to exchange the old garment for a new one. This was done under duress and trepidation, for supply sergeants don't like to part with anything, but will accept any and every kind of equipment.

Several days later, the company executive officer punished me for an act of soldier snobbery. I was assigned to dig a fox hole 4' x 6' x 2' with a table spoon in the sandy soil on the side of the barracks and sleep in it that night. A guard checked on my presence every hour, on his appointed rounds. In the morning, I had to fill the fox hole with the same spoon and report to the lieutenant. This is army chicken _ _ _ _ again! I was an infidel in the holy temple of soldiering.

My mortar squad was operating at an efficient level, the best in the company, for setting up and for firing the weapon, but little ammunition was available. To get used to the weight of the rounds of non-existent ammunition on marches, we loaded our field packs with the equivalency of rocks. I was promoted to staff sergeant and the two gunners became P.F.C.'s. We thought we were big shots. I memorized the firing tables and invented a sighting device, which I never disclosed to anyone because it wasn't an army approved device and I used it in combat, effectively. It saved ammunition.

Several parachute jumps were made to practice assembly techniques and to satisfy the requirement for jump pay. Experiments were to be unleashed as new assembly plans were designed. The techniques and those who experimented with them were called pathfinders. Some regiments asked for volunteers, and company commanders found this to be a good way to get rid of those who wouldn't soldier by the rules. The pathfinders were a group who were to precede the main body of an airborne invasion by setting

Trial by Combat

up, on the drop zone, a lighted "T" guiding the incoming flights of jumpers which were in sections of 45 planes each, in the formation of a V of V's. An instrument called "Eureka" located at the end of a long leg of the 'T', emitted a Morse code signal in dots and dashes identifying the drop zone-A, B, C and D. The lead aircraft of a section of the incoming flight had a receiving instrument called "Rebecca." The flight leader would hone in on the emitted signal from Eureka at distance of 20 miles and would fly up the long leg of the "T." When it crossed the horizontal leg of the "T" the green GO light signaled the jumpers in motion. At the same time the six parapacks slung under the belly of the aircraft were released, manually and electrically by jumpers numbers 2 and 3. This procedure was refined to drop 13, 200 paratroopers of the 82 nd and 101st Airborne Divisions on June 6, 1944, at Normandy, France, the Cross-Channel attack; Operation Overlord; and Operation Market-Garden in the Netherlands on September 17, 1944.

During the maneuvers, the Tennessee dirt farmers were always on the look-out for a good economic venture, which they found in the sale of stale candy bars and other goodies of the South, to the marching soldiers along the decomposed granite roads in the countryside. During an early morning halt, my squad was invited to a ham and egg breakfast in an old ramshackle farm house during a seasonal rain storm. We were hungry, wet, and with delight we accepted the invitation, except me, for what reason I can't remember, maybe because there was not enough room for the entire squad and equipment in the farm house. I felt that someone had to give the squad a warning when the company was ready to move out, so I If we left the equipment outside it would give away our absence in the company formation. I stood guard in the woods at a distance to watch and warn. The bipod of the mortar was placed on the running board of an old Model T Ford in front of the house. The heavy steel base plate and the firing tube were carried into the farm house. Let the Tennessee Maneuvers proceed, for now it was time to eat. Here and now, we had a chance dry out and eat and get real warm. Unknown to us, outside a strange event was escalating into a regrettable situation for which the squad would dearly pay. When breakfast was finished and the squad came out of the farm house.

The Model T Ford was nowhere to be found. We didn't hear it leave. The bipod was gone which was an expensive item and rendered the mortar accuracy less than desirable. We marched on and joined the company. The assistant gunner decided that without the heavy steel base plate and the bipod the firing tube was useless, and as we crossed a small stone bridge, the gunner tossed the base plate, the heaviest part, into the stream without my knowledge. Now all that was left of our weapon was the firing tube, the sighting device and a few rounds of ammunition. Our load was lighter. Now that war games in Tennessee were over, Colonel Johnson was elated, but felt there was a need for fine tuning. We returned to Camp MacKall and prepared for an experimental jump using a squad of pathfinders

To airlift a regiment from an airport to a drop zone, a series of pathfinders were needed to mark the way on the ground, with bright red panels of orange colored smoke. The pathfinders would be dropped at intervals, in pairs, before the regiment flew in the direction of the drop zone. The pathfinders would, upon sighting the in coming flight, setoff the smoke signal. A gigantic display would occur on the drop zone. The pathfinder teams were to avoid being captured by the red army defenders during the parachute maneuvers. Three of us were parachuted on the drop zone at dusk to reconnoiter the area and clear it of any enemy by leading them on a stray route to anywhere. We set off orange smoke signals at 8:00 a. m. or at the first sound or sight of the air armada. They flew in sections and the formation of V of V's. I stood in the middle of the drop zone and fired off several orange smoke canisters and threw them in compass directions. This would the procedure for the morning.

Now let's go back to the previous afternoon; one drop zone pathfinder aircraft flew over the drop zone at 700 feet on target, and we jumped. Each of us landed in nearby pine trees without injury. We found our parapack bundles which contained all of our equipment, hid our parachutes under pine needles and boughs. We carefully prowled the drop zone so as not to be seen by any enemy patrols. If we were captured there would be no drop zone signals and we would have a short trip to jail. While patrolling, we found several luscious watermelon patches in adjacent fields and carefully loaded our backpacks with excellent choices and returned to our

Trial by Combat

secluded landing spot We dug holes to hide them until the early hours of the morning. We were going to distribute them to our squad members. A red army patrol came through the area in the early hours of darkness, oblivious of our presence and plan, but on the lookout. Our camouflage of pine needles and pine boughs was good enough that the patrol scrambled through the vegetation and entanglements. Upon hearing their non-intellectual conversation, we jumped out of our hiding, only in our camouflage underwear and jump boots, and led the enemy patrol on a wild scramble through the woods like jackrabbits, and circled back to our warren. The rest of the darkness of the night and the light of the morning passed without incident.

At 8:00 A.M., the first sight and sound told us that the air armada was on target. I was in an incomplete uniform, in the center of the drop zone with four orange smoke grenades, to be thrown in four different directions. As the colored smoke engulfed the pastoral scene, the low flying C-47's began to disgorge their human cargo. The jumpers looked like a steady stream of unraveling colored nylon as they floated down, in a windless atmosphere. I stood like a statue and watched everything falling from the sky around me: multicolored parachutes from which swung pieces of 75 mm artillery cannon, camouflage parachutes guiding thousands of armed paratroopers safely to the ground, and equipment bundles of ammunition with machine guns. An officer landed in front of me, and since I was half naked, said to me, "Soldier, get your clothes on, the General will be here any moment." Again they were pouring out of the aircraft in a steady stream, layer upon layer of paratroopers descending in the same air space where collisions and malfunctions were possible. One jumper exited the airplane in bad body position and got his feet tangled in his suspension lines and landed on the canopy below him. He was unable to walk off of the parachute as it gave way under his weight. As the parachute oscillated, he slid off and was caught by the jumper whose parachute he had invaded, only two hundred feet from the ground. They made a hard landing, with only minor injuries. A life was saved by quick thinking. He was awarded a soldier's medal.

Thomas M. Rice

Troops assembled on each side of the perimeter of the drop zone by companies A, B, C, and Headquarters company, guided by the whirring clarion, sounds of bugles, shrill whistles and sirens. After the men retrieved their equipment, I distributed the stolen hidden watermelons from the raid the night before to the members of the squad, for who knew when and where the next meal would come.

The regiment, under a tactical exercise, prepared for an attack on the objective and the red army enemy. This last exercise ended several days later after the enemy was declared shattered by the observing officials. The Tennessee dirt farmers were always on the look-out for a good economic venture. That night the squad bedded down in the open fields of a farm. The hay had been harvested and piled in a very large and high stack near the farm house. Needing warmth and comfort, the squad raided the hay stack, scattered the hay in small piles throughout the field, as one-man accommodations. The farmer wasn't aware of the scattering of his hay stack until light of day. During an early morning battle order, we moved out with great speed. My mortar sighting device was nowhere to be found. The farmer was under suspicion as the thief. The mortar sight turned up as a sale item back to the army and the farmer had his revenge for our raid on his hay. There was a raid on his chicken coop by one of the other company men which resulted in a feast. The chaplain was even deviled into devouring the chicken parts. The farmer's complaint ultimately reached Colonel Johnson and he ordered a fine of several dollars for each officer and a fine of coins for each enlisted man.

We returned to Camp MacKall five weeks and five exercises later, and continued with similar exercises. which 'fine tuned' us to a very efficient level. We were ready for overseas shipment, so they told us. We were proficient.

After the exercises were concluded, equipment up-graded, replacements of men who were injured or who otherwise failed in any other way, joined the plaroons. The regiment continued to build military efficiency up to the divisional level. The final series of exercises had been the Tennessee Maneuvers and were concluded. This was the final test of combat efficiency, rain or shine. All went well and the 101 st Airborne Division was declared combat ready.

At the platoon and squad level, we were getting tired, hungry, and ready for a furlough.

When the maneuvers had ended company C had assembled at Camp MacKall with the 501st regiment. Training and evaluation continued. The essential pieces of the mortar missing? The mortar squad certainly looked strange in company formation. The so-called theft was reported by me, and Captain Phillips called me into his office for a hearing and an appropriate remedy of the situation. The remedy started with the reading of the Articles of War and the care and cleaning of government property. The gunner was given the same treatment by the captain even though our cases were heard on an individual basis. The next penalty was the application of a fine for the cost of the equipment. My fine for the mortar sight was $36.00. I never asked the gunner, Frank Ficarotta, what his fine was. Soon we had a new and complete mortar delivered to the squad from Ordnance company. If this had occurred during war time under combat conditions, nothing would have been said and I could have found a replacement with ease.

There occurred in the company, from time to time, a rash of A.W.O.L's (absent without official leave) while we were fine tuning our training for combat. We were using live ammunition for realism. New techniques of marching fire power were being practiced, and every man's presence was vital to the war effort. One paratrooper, Charles Bowman, was declared absent without official leave. He was located several days later in a Philadelphia military jail. Thomas M. Rice and Myron G. Sessions were detailed to return him to his unit. Special orders were cut and the personal guards were on their way to Philadelphia. Bowman was handcuffed at all times so that he would not attempt an escape, even in the bathroom. Bowman was required to pay all expenses of food and transportation. His extended punishment was not known, but he disappeared from the ranks. He was drummed out.

A few recruits reported from time to time, and company C received its share, as some of the originals disqualified themselves by some prohibitive act. Another incident brought the regiment to the edge of shame. A young woman had been raped and there were no obvious suspects. The entire regiment was assembled on the parade field, and the young woman was seated in a command car behind a tinted windshield to protect her identity. One by one each paratrooper in the regiment marched from company formation and stood at attention in front of the command car and was waved away if not recognized by the young woman. No positive identification was made in the entire regiment. This was one of the most humiliating affairs during my entire military service. An officer was under suspicion.

Charlotte, North Carolina, was a favorite hang-out for the 501st Parachute Infantry Regiment as well as the 502nd, 506th Regiments and the Nissie 441st Infantry Regiment (Japanese - American second generation.) There always was an exhibition of "who is the best" between paratrooper infantry, armored units and other regular infantry units that emanated from bars and other dens of iniquity. These confrontations always manifested themselves out in the streets as center stage affairs which required the military police to quell the uprising. The Charlotte riot was a deep penetrating affair, and the main weapon was judo. The repercussions went all the way to 1600 Pennsylvania avenue, Washington D.C. for a final decision. Charlotte, North Carolina was declared off limits for three months for all airborne regiments. Colonel Johnson, our regimental commander, never forgave us for his military embarrassment and frequently admonished us again and again for it. His final words, on his battle field death in Holland, to Colonel Kinnard, were, "Take care of my boys." He forgave us at last.[1]

Fall weather was drawing to a close and the regiment had not made the long anticipated move to a port of embarkation as had the 502nd and the 506th PIR. The troops were getting restless. The Colonel, for a diversion, selected a goat for a mascot. The 506 th regiment had also done so and had their mascot jump trained. Our goat was a beer swilling shabby animal. Why of course it had to be jump trained so as not to be outdone by the 506 regiment. A harness was designed and fitted for "Geronimo." He was airlifted to 1200 feet but refused to jump. Several flights over the drop zone

---

1 His final words on his battlefield death in Holland, to Colonels Kinnard and Ewell were, "Take care of my boys." He forgave us at last. Sampson, Lookout Below, p.ge 27.

Trial by Combat

produced no success. The four jump masters couldn't get him out of the door. It seems that we had a failure to communicate with this smelly beast. We thought he was cowardly for not jumping; he thought we were stupid for jumping. When Colonel Johnson heard of Geronimo's unacceptable conduct, he drummed the goat out of the regiment. Have you ever seen a drunken goat weaving on the two right legs and then on the two left legs? This was the condition in which we left Geronimo at Camp MacKall. Next, Colonel Johnson adopted a cub bear. Before the bear could be jump-trained, it escaped and we were alerted to overseas shipment. The regiment that replaced us in our old quarters found a rather large bear coming out of hibernation.[2]

It was a summer of thunder at Camp MacKall, after the Tennessee maneuvers and before we were sent to Camp Miles Standish near Boston for overseas shipment. At the conclusion of a long conditioning hike, part of which was at double time with full field pack and weapons, the regiment took a needed rest at the dam of a man-made lake. The perimeter of the lake was about one mile and had a very steep shore line. Each of us was required to jump into the water with all of our equipment and struggle to shore without losing our weapon. Only a few rescues were made for those who didn't know how to swim. After everyone completed this exercise, part of the lake was doused with gasoline and ignited. We were again required to jump into the flaming waters without equipment, return to the surface, splash the flames away and swim to safety. This was more disarming than one would think, but it was a ship board exercise in case we were torpedoed in the Atlantic Ocean en route to England. It was a good way to cool off after the forced march. Never again did we repeat this.

After training and several months of slow motion idleness, we were alerted for overseas shipment in December, 1943. It was thought by high command that the regiment wasn't ready because of so much slack time and an inordinate number of A.W.O.L's and

---

2 Colonel Johnson adopted a bear cub. Before the bear could be jump- trained it escaped and we were alerted to overseas shipment. The regiment that replaced us in our old quarters found a rather large bear coming out of hibernation. Ibid, pge.29-30.

V D cases. The 101st Airborne Division hadn't been brought to full combat strength until the 501st Parachute Infantry Regiment was attached. The 501st was the last regiment to train as an organized unit.[3] The 502nd and the 506th regiments had finished jump training and were combat ready. They were the first to arrive in England and the 501 was the last to arrive. We were tired of training and wanted to get overseas and get the job done. We were also beginning to feel useless, for up to this point we had had no real part in the war. When that happened, the morale went down and we were looking for trouble, even if we had to manufacture it. To counter this, strong disciplinary measures were in place; then the obedience factor hits rock bottom. It didn't take Colonel Johnson long to realize this slump. The long pep talks and speeches by the colonel became muted because the men were more mature and resented the call-to-goodness. He realized he had gone too far when he got no response from his high pitched emotion. When he screamed, "What are we here for?" instead of answering with the usual acceptance, "To fight," We roared back, "Furlough." We fell out of his reasoning pattern. For the first time the colonel was desolate, scared and afraid that the fighting edge would be dulled by apathy and indifference. The colonel concluded that "morale is a mighty force as vital as the materials of war themselves.

The Colonel spoke, (He tried to review our developmental training experiences from Camp Toccoa to Camp MacKall):

> "Fellow Geronimos, We are about to start a new training phase since all of you have successfully completed basic and jump training phases. You have demonstrated beyond a shadow of doubt the marked possibility of superior individual performance that is possessed by members of this organization. The current training will stress unit training, that is, the training of the squad, the platoon, the company, the battalion, and finally the regiment to function as a smooth efficient team in combat. A team that will

---

3 The 501st was the last regiment to train as an organized unit. Rapport and Northwood, <u>Rendezvous With Destiny</u>, pge. 45.

Trial by Combat

be so perfect in its weapon techniques and so skilled in its tactical techniques that it repeatedly strikes devastating blows to its enemies with minimum loss to ourselves.

In order to weld a smart hard hitting team, that will strike terror into the hearts of our enemies, we must have the whole -hearted cooperation of every last man in this regiment. Remember, we are here for one purpose and only one purpose: to prepare for successful combat. You must be so superbly trained that it will be the enemies' blood that will run in pools, not yours. (Colonel Johnson was referring to General Patton's statement, when he said, " A pint of sweat will save a gallon of blood.") Every individual in this regiment can greatly assist or hinder us in the successful accomplishment of our mission. Every A.W.O.L., every venereal, every court marshal and every display of gangsterism is a direct assist on the part of the offender to the axis cause. These offenses tend to hamper training and hurt the good name of the regiment. We don't believe in guard houses or court marshals in this organization; you are selected men and so are your officers; don't force us to resort to such methods to maintain discipline, get the spirit of cooperation and team work during this training period. Every soldier or unit you see in camp or in the surrounding area is a perspective buddy in combat. Men of other organizations and battalions may look mighty good to you some day when you are in a tough spot. Get acquainted with them for you all have a mutual objective, to beat the axis rats thoroughly and decisively and return to your peaceful pursuits in a democratic nation once again. Time is working against us; we may be called sooner than we anticipate. You are all anxious for combat but remember you must be skilled before you can be successful. Give your best during this period and we will turn out a fighting regiment that will make the name of Geronimo and it's motto, 'Strike and destroy' known throughout the civilized world.

Remember-we are the Rome, Berlin, and Tokyo express. Are you ready? Let's go! Geronimo!!!"[4]

Our ears were full of the clamor and noise of the world of civilians and we failed to hear Colonel Johnson's stirring words, but if we were honest we would have prefered our bold whims to his groveling high pitched voice. We were not allowed to abdicate and follow our own leadings, for it is time for combat. We were yearning for the miracle of fire. I believe the colonel talked to us as if to baptize the ground we were to land on in France.

Sooner or later, the regiment would be involved in a complicated process known as P.O.M., or preparation for overseas movements.[5] Short furloughs were given, and upon our return to Camp MacKall, we were sent by train to Camp Miles Standish near Boston. Camp Miles Standish was the same for everybody, a filthy stink hole with little sanitation, a succession of inspections, inoculations, lectures, and packing and unpacking our equipment. As the regiment gathered in a large assembly hall to listen to a lecture on the use of an anti-gas ointment, the lecturing lieutenant proceeded to tell us that the gas ointment should be applied to the soles and the sides of each foot and then the socks are to be put on. If this had been done our feet would have been blistered. The only place you apply the ointment is on the outside of the combat boots. Before the lieutenant had put a period at the end of his last sentence, a colonel intervened and dismissed the lieutenant from the stage and corrected his misguided information. This drew loud cheers and whistles. It sounded like the Assyria came down like the wolf on the fold with his cohorts gleaming in purple and gold. Security measures in the camp were

---

[4] "Strike and destroy" known throughout the civilized world. Remember we are known as the Rome, Berlin and Tokyo express. Sampson, Lookout Below, pge. 37.

[5] Sooner or later the regiment would be involved in a complicated process known as P.O.M. or preparation for overseas movement. Kennett, GI The American Soldier, pge.111.

Trial by Combat

strict. All identifying marks of regiments were obliterated and replaced by shipping code numbers. None of us had "gang plank fever;" we were ready, eager and anxious to go. We shipped out to the European Theater of Operations on board the army transport SS WILLIAM G. GOETHALS for a twelve day zig zag transatlantic convoyed crossing, December 19, 1943. En route to Britain, we were issued a Short Guide to Great Britain, 38 page handbook written by Eric Knight. We arrived at Glascow, Scotland, January 1, 1944. This ended the chapter about our final training in the United States, and we were glad to be on our way to England where we felt we would make the final preparation for combat. There was, however, an incident that occurred while we were at Camp MacKall, which is worth telling, but not worth bragging about. It came to be known as the Charlotte Riots. No one knew for certain how the riots really started, but there were several different versions.

A moldy old story, deeply etched in the minds of the participants, was on the cutting edge of being retold time and time again, but there were no listeners. Year after year, the reunioning paratroopers of the 501st Parachute Infantry Regiment were eager to relive the Battle of Charlotte in 1943, but no one came forward or no one who knows anything was present at the reunion and the subject wasn't brought up until 1998.

Everyone who was at Camp MacKall after the Tennessee Maneuvers, remembers the aftermath of the riot. It was Charlotte recaptured. The aftermath brought down on the regiment by a General, was a series of ever-increasing admonitions:
1. Airborne units were banned from Charlotte, North Carolina for a period of three months or until we were sent overseas.
2. A threatened loss of our jump boots.
3. A thorough grilling by Colonel Johnson in regimental formation.
4. Unknown extension of restrictions, not revealed.

No one knew exactly how the riot really started. It was building towards a final confrontation over a period of many months as to "Who was the best." The pent - up energies that we all had stored up during the Tennessee Maneuvers needed a quick-release valve. We had the money and we knew Charlotte and we knew exactly where its watering holes were located, and so did the 444st Hawaiian Regimental Combat Team. It was the Crystal Cafe.

The paratroop regimental policy for quick energy release decreed that the men of any company completing a full month of training without anybody going A.W.O.L., coming down with V.D. or failing to qualify on the rifle range would be given a three day pass.

George Koumalat of company E stepped forward during the 1998 reunion and told Bill Sefton of Regimental Headquarters just how it all started. He said that he had struck the first blow.

We were all back at Camp MacKall after five weeks of the Tennessee Maneuvers, and had a loud jingle in our pockets. George and four of his company E buddies took off for the well known haunts of Charlotte, after having massed eighteen days of regimental rewards. Upon their arrival at their favorite den of iniquity, they found it occupied predominately by the 441st Hawaiian soldiers ("Go for broke") and their southern belles, who exclaimed, "Oh look!, the paratroopers are back," and the belles proceeded to abandon the Hawaiians.

One misguided Hawaiian soldier, disturbed by the desertion of his date, gravitated toward George and his enclave of four, to retrieve her. George was sufficiently offended to clobber the soldier with one punch and the battle was on. The Hawaiian buddies sought revenge on the odd-numbered paratroopers. The fight spread from bar to bar throughout Charlotte with Hawaiians being joined by some civilians with anti-airborne sentiment. The shouts of "Geronimo" were probably heard throughout the city, as the combatants engaged each other with judo chops as front stage affairs, in the streets and on the corners.

The M.P.'s were called to the fray and were hauling scores of embittered and embattled Geronimos to the local jail, only to find that the jail was overcrowded. They were released and told to leave town.

According to George, his group was jailed five times, and they returned each time to the fun of fighting, before realizing that there would be serious consequences if they stayed to fight. They commandeered a taxi cab and hired the driver to take them to

Trial by Combat

Southern Pines. Upon arrival, they paid the driver one half of what they considered an unreasonable rate. They departed briskly and hid out near the railroad station until dark. The cabby soon complained to the police and the five could hear the police car sirens searching in the area for them.

The station closed at dark because the only train to come through was a non-stop to Washington, D.C. Determined to get out of town, they stole a lantern from inside the depot and flagged the train, boarded it, and convinced the conductor to let them pay the fare to Washington.

They spent the next two weeks playing tourist with female companionship. Finally returning to Camp MacKall, they were stopped at the gate by the M.P.'s who assumed they were A.W.O.L. and called regimental headquarters. Colonel Johnson came to the gate himself, verified that the passes were valid and complimented them on their good judgment to enjoy the rich historical and cultural environs of Washington, instead of the dens of iniquity in Charlotte.[6]

They slipped right through the clinched fist of Colonel Johnson as their sobriety was never questioned. The statute of limitations had long since expired. They were all home free. This was their finest hour. If all of the undisciplined and roughnecks had been formed up in one battalion, what would the 501 P I R be like, in garrison and in combat? Goebells, if asked, would say, "All they need is a dagger." There was another group called the "Filthy 13." Adventures unknown, story never told, end of history. This is only one version of the Battle of Charlotte, North Carolina.

ANOTHER KEYSTONE RENDITION

Company G of the 501 PIR arrived at Camp MacKall, North Carolina from Fort Benning, Georgia after completing jump school.

---

[6] Colonel Johnson came to the gate himself, verified that the passes were valid, and complimented them on their good judgment to enjoy the rich historical and cultural environs of Washington, D.C. instead of the dens of iniquity of Charlotte. Sefton, Geronimo Newsletter, Winter, 1998.

It was located on a corner almost directly across the street from the telephone exchange.

This seemed like a dream almost come true as the young female telephone operators were quartered on the second floor of the building. The elation didn't last long as a detachment of Hawaiian troops were brought in to locate tents immediately beside the exchange building. They must have been on some sort of special service. All they had to do was whitewash a stone border around their area, grow flowers, strum ukeleles and warble day and night.

Soon the Company G troopers began to bitch to the 501st PIR cadre First Sergeant Dean C, Swem that the noise was keeping them awake at night. They had some justification in their griping. The training schedule was particularly rigorous with prolonged calisthenics and a 10 to 25 mile road march with full field packs day or night. What the tired troopers didn't need was Hawaiian ukulele serenades during the few hours of sleep they managed to get. Therefore, there was a lot of unflattering language and gestures being exchanged across the road. The telephone operators loved all the attention from the Hawaiian soldiers and sentimental syrupy ballads that ran on and on. Needless to say, there was considerable animosity that developed between the two bodies of troops.

Charlotte, North Carolina was considered a favorite city for week-end passes. It also happened that a rangy muscular paratrooper named Kenneth Beal of Company G chose to visit Charlotte on one week-end. He was quiet, disciplined, a hard and willing trooper never known to cause any sort of trouble. But Beal chose to visit a favorite watering hole for military personnel. As he entered, he walked by a booth where several of the Hawaiian soldiers were seated. One smart-assed Hawaiian stuck out his foot and tripped the unsuspecting Beal. He fell heavily on the floor as the Hawaiians howled with delight. That didn't last long. Beal got up and continued to another booth on the same side and ordered a beer. He drank slowly and thoughtfully and made a decision. He dropped to the floor under the booths, crawled back to the ones where the Hawaiians were, got under the table, rose up and sent the beer and glasses flying. All of this didn't go unobserved by many other troopers who were sympathetic to poor Beal.

Trial by Combat

As the Hawaiians struggled to regain their balance, they grabbed Beal and started to work him over. That did it! A free for all was on and spread outside and into the street. More troopers began to get involved and the situation became a small riot. MP's and local police soon arrived; the latter got the melee under control.

The following Monday morning produced a unusual regimental formation. Colonel Howard "Geronimo" Johnson took the stand. He began with,

> Men, the 501st is disgraced again.
> I thought that caper in Atlanta was bad. but that paled by comparison.
> You aren't acting like good paratroopers, but like a mindless rabble.
> You men have been accused of inciting a riot in Charlotte. From now on that city is off-limits to this regiment. Any one caught going there will face severe discipline.
> You have brought untold dishonor and disgrace to the 501st.

By this time he had worked himself into a frenzy, hopping up and down, waving his arms, and his face as red as a baboon's ass. He looked like a candidate for an apoplectic fit or a stroke. He yelled a troop dismissal and the stunned officers and men of the regiment formed up and moved out to their respective company areas.

Yes, the 501st PIR was in disgrace. The Colonel had the regimental flag flown at half-mast at the headquarters. The Geronimo Journal came out with a black border all around the front page. The Charlotte Observer came out Sunday with huge banner black headlines. No one dared to think of going to Charlotte on pass.

There was an upside to all this. The Hawaiians shut-up. The troopers began to date the telephone exchange girls. The tensions eased off and there was some humor in 'Old Geronimo's war dance.

The training schedule got tougher, whether it was from the effects of the riot or just a natural progression. It made no difference to the line troopers who endured it all.

How did Swem know all this? Pvt. Beal, that honest individual, told him when he came into the orderly room from a pass with two black eyes, a battered face, and a uniform in disarray. Swem was also present at the formation when Colonel Johnson went on his rampage and what followed.[7]

I asked S/Sgt Sessions what he knew of the Charlotte Affair, either one version or both versions. He whimsically replied, "I slept through the whole action. I am glad I wasn't there or I might have gotten bloodied." Frank Carpenter and I were still on the road hitch-hiking to Charlotte at that time. The city was quiet after that, so we had our Chinese chop suey dinner in peace and quiet at our favorite restaurant.

---

[7] How did Swem know all this? Swem was present at the formation when Colonel Johnson went on his rampage.<u>Geronimo Newsletter</u>, June, 1999. pges.16-17.

Chapter 7

Overseas - England

A day without a crisis is a total loss.

    My sea voyage was an uneventful cascade of pain, desolation, and confinement to the ship's hospital isolation ward just below the main deck. I had the mumps on both sides of my jaw. No visitors were allowed but, I had a clean bed with white sheets and aching jaws. During the early morning hours, I was awakened by the rhythmical cadence of physical exercises of the men just above me. The side straddles hops were easily identified. There was little room for the men to exercise in unison, so the companies had to take turns on an hourly basis. The cadence went on most of the morning. Two meals were served a day and salt water showers were the order of the day, with salt water G I soap. A few preferred to stay in the hot steamy hold of the rolling ship and to exit on occasion for a deep breath of fresh air and to see the sights of the convoy. Who cares where we are! It takes a load of optimism to find happiness on a troop transport for twelve days en route to the war zone.
    Colonel Johnson took a personal hand in training a .50 caliber gun crew for anti-aircraft defense. Half-way across the Atlantic Ocean, he called the entire regiment on deck to witness the gun crew's expertise. A weather balloon inflated with helium, about eight feet in diameter, was the target. When it was released from the

deck, Johnson restrained the gun crew fire "Hold your fire! Hold your fire!" When it was about 1000 feet in the air, "Shoot 'er down!" he shouted. The gun - crew fired and fired until the balloon was finally lost in sight, without a hit amid the boos and laughter that seemed to drive the target higher and faster.[1]

The many uneventful days and nights passed for the paratroopers en route, including the merchant marine crew, who could be seen at night chomping on their steak and potatoes, which galled the spam-oppressed 501st paratroopers.

When the ship docked at Glasgow, Scotland, I was the first one taken ashore on a stretcher to a U.S. Army hospital. I was there for 10 days. After the quarantine expired, I took 10 airborne men to their assigned parachute units of the 101st Airborne Division area (see map) which formed a rectangle in a westerly direction from London. Along this east-west axis from Reading, Newbury, and Swindon were scattered the regiments of the division. Lambourne was a small village in the Cotswold horse hills region. The verdant rolling hills gave a peaceful and serene atmosphere to the military training. Company C was quartered on the monastery grounds, which were surrounded by antiquity. Our quarters, within the monastery walls, were 5 Nissan huts roofed with curved corrugated steel. One hundred twenty eight parachutists lived there for five months. The huts were arranged in somewhat of a semi-circle, which was surrounded by ten foot high walls of 15th century antiquity. It was soon discovered by the more enterprising soldiers that there was a series of underground tunnels from the monastery grounds to the cemetery and church, which ultimately led to a cave of catacombs. The tunnels were soon blocked off because of the risk of a cave - in. This ended our exploration of the 16th century church artifacts. The townspeople of Lambourne and the religious clerics never knew of our underground intrusion into their ancestral heritage.

The first few weeks of activities in England were low key because the parachutists of the 101st Airborne division were not acknowledged nor identified as having arrived in the United

---

1 "Hold your fire, hold your fire." Bando, <u>101st Airborne Division At Normandy,</u> pge.12.

Trial by Combat

Kingdom. We came dressed as ordinary infantrymen. We became accustomed to our barracks (huts), weather (fog), but we missed many things such as maple syrup, tomato catsup, and T- bone steaks, but we were never short of cabbage or Brussels sprouts. One of the locally produced items that many G I's liked was denied to us. We were forbidden to drink unpasteurized milk because it was a serious health hazard (mad cow disease). What we did was to slink out of the compound and up to a farm house door and ask for milk. If we didn't do that we would find a cow and milk it. With the canteen cup full, we raced for the barracks to make hot chocolate or cocoa.[2] One British item that I favored was fish and chips, wrapped in a hot newspaper. When tensions flared paratroopers fought over girls, money and beer. We were incredibly generous with money, but in a pub we went crazy the way we threw cash around. A favorite trick was to bite a glass in half and accuse the bartender of poor quality glassware and beer, because it was warm. The taste of Britain was Brussels sprouts, mutton, boiled potatoes, strong tea, with a dash of heavy dark bread called the National Loaf[3]. We viewed films and listened to orientation talks on how to get along with the British, and finally a new monetary system of pounds, shillings, and pence, which came easy because we want to spend our jump pay, on what, who knows? We found British money meaningless "monopoly money." We were irritated by the size of the five pound note termed- "wallpaper."[4] Our physical setup wasn't out of the ordinary. The Nissan steel huts were dark and gloomy, with no way to improve them. The floors were concrete and dusty. Double bunks were in rows from one end of the hut to the other, leaving a center aisle. We slept on straw and excelsior packing material mattresses. We covered ourselves with two thin olive drab blankets that were scratchy to the skin. I used a second mattress cover as a sheet, like a sleeping bag, and crawled in between. Small pot-bellied stoves provided a small

---

2 We were forbidden to drink unpasteurized milk because it was a serious health hazard, Gardiner, Overseas, Overpaid, Over here, pge.38.
3 The taste of Britain was of Brussels sprouts, mutton, boiled potatoes, strong tea, with a dash of heavy dark bread called the 'National loaf'.Ibid, pge.132.
4 We found British money meaningless - 'monopoly money'.We were irritated by the size of the five pound note termed -'wallpaper'.Ibid, pge.33.

semblance of heat from stolen coal. Sanitary conditions left much to be desired. It looked like Camp Miles Standish all over again. Our toilets were housed in an open air shanty with several stone troughs for urinating, and several rows of wooden seats perched on honey buckets. The toilet paper was not always available, but when it was it was of a course brown texture and stamped "U S Army Property." The latrine had no place to stand and converse at night. The shower and wash rooms were satisfactory for they had to serve a company of 128 men at a fast rate. There was usually enough hot water if the Charge of Quarters was paying attention to his first morning duty which was to keep the fires burning under the water tanks. Frank Carpenter forgot to stoke the boilers, and consequently one morning, there was no hot water. The first sergeant never forgot Carpenter's malfeasance Frank was never promoted above the rank of corporal. This is what we called "chicken shit." We washed our hands and faces and shaved in our helmets with hot water. We looked on our life in the United States as luxurious.

Our diet, so rich in staples such as milk and eggs, fruit, suddenly dried up; we ate powdered eggs, powdered milk, dehydrated apricots, fruit cocktail by the canteen cup full and don't forget dehydrated potatoes, which were as hard as granite unless soaked for hours. We were subject to a constant diet of spam immersed in grease. All P.X. goods were rationed on a weekly basis and consisted of seven packs of unknown cigarette brands, three candy bars any kind, one cake of soap, one box of matches, one package of razor blades, wash rags, towels, combs and coat hangers.

After the company was settled and comfortable with Anglo-American relations relaxed, we went exploring for everything in neighboring towns and villages, near and far. Railroad transportation was free, if you were in uniform. There was nothing else to wear. We had nothing else except a jingle in our pockets. We were over-paid, over-sexed and over-here. It was soon recognized that the recent arrival of paratroopers and little known British sex habits had caused the bed springs to become worn from passion.

The language was easy enough and different enough to be fun- British speech. One week-end I traveled on the London - Midland - Scottish train to a nearby village, just to see the sights and enjoy

Trial by Combat

the country-side and the architectural wonders of England. On the return train trip to Lambourne (our barracks), a Women's Land Army woman (W.L.A.) boarded and entered the compartment that I was in. We struck up a long conversation about something I can't remember. The only thing I do remember was that she invited me to come home with her until I had to report for duty the next day. In my stupidity I told her that I wasn't able to do so because I didn't have my toothbrush and a pair of pajamas. Today, I still wonder what in the hell I was thinking, and upon what basis I gave her a flabbergasted answer.

The airborne troops offered parties, glamour, dances, treats, luxuries, romance, and fun every week-end, at a time of loneliness and drab austerity. For the older women, there was a substitute son, for the younger British soldier the American G.I. was a threat-over-paid, over-sexed, over-here. We responded with under-paid, under-sexed, and under-fed, which had a ring of truth.[5] The most disliked American trait for the British was boastfulness. Americans are like large dogs trying to be friendly with everyone in the room, while wrecking everything with their wagging tail. If you are invited to a British home and the host exhorts you to "Eat up, there is plenty on the table, "it may be all the family rations for a whole week, spread out to show their hospitality. After many years of war, the British were ashamed of their meager rations: a 3 oz. ration of cheese, cut into tiny cubes, 2 oz. of butter spread thinly across the national loaf, and drab threadbare homes.[6]

When the 501st Parachute Infantry landed in England, we made the mistake of thinking that because we spoke the same language, the English were just like ourselves. We expected a home away from home and what we found was a foreign country;[7] and from their food we got severe constipation.

Training for the invasion was at hand. The 101 st Airborne division had had now been identified because our division insignia

---

5 For the older women there was a substitute son, for the younger British soldier the American G.I. was threat-overpaid, oversexed, over here, Ibid, pge.55.
6 The British were ashamed of their meager rations. Ibid, pge.132.
7 We expected a home away from home but what we found was a foreign country. Gardiner, Ibid, pge. 38.

73

has been sewn on our left shoulder and our pants were bloused in our jump boots. Our presence in the U.K. became well-known as we traveled about on the week-ends. Axis Sally, a well known traitor, broadcast American and big band music from Germany, gave us recognition in the form of a stern warning when she announced during one of her overseas broadcasts that " We know the 501st Parachute Infantry Regiment is in the United Kingdom and if you don't believe this, go out in the village square and look at the village clock. "It is two minutes slow." she announced the correct time and concluded with this ominous warning, " We have just finished painting two thousand crosses white and we are waiting for you." One of our instructions for D - Day was "to take no prisoners."[8] Again, Axis sally, Mildred Gillars, made us sit up in our beds and listen: "All right you paratroopers, we know you are going to jump into Southern France and we have a welcome party waiting for you," Gillars cooed in her perfect sultry English "Oh, by the way, you don't need to bring your parachutes, you will be able to walk down from the sky on our flak." Men may boast about what you say, but they will believe what you will do.[9]

There were a number of brawls with the air force men in the village pubs. Fines were assessed for knifing private reserve deer on Lady Craven's estate. We climbed trees and leaped upon deer.with knife in hand. We blew up her trout streams with hand grenades. Prostitutes infiltrated our regimental areas at night. Lady Craven never knew of this caper.

Special training missions hadn't been assigned for the cross-channel attack but a program of physical conditioning, airborne tactics, small unit (squad) leadership training began, whereby a private became a squad leader through the field problem as we went over hill and dale through barbed wire pastures to capture the objective. The farmers resented our trampling through their wheat fields. Each platoon was assigned two platoon officers because of the anticipated casualties in combat. Jumping was very hazardous.[10]

---

8 take no prisoners, Cartlege, <u>Unpublished Manuscript,</u> pge.7.
9 "Oh, by the way, you don't need to bring your parachutes. You will be able to walk down from the sky on our flak." <u>Ibid,</u> pge.7.
10 Jumping was a real hazard. Sampson, <u>Lookout Below,</u> pge. 10.

Trial by Combat

We trained six days a week for forty-eight hours. Company C marched 15, 18, 21 miles during the training periods, one hour of close combat with trench knives, eight hours of night operations. Some variety was introduced with street fighting, map reading, first aid, and chemical warfare training. I had to supervise the company through a tear gas exercise with and without gas masks. The only military custom that was abandoned was close order drill.

A number of training courses were organized. I was sent to the British 6th Parachute Regiment for two weeks to exchange places with a British para to gain new ideas about their weapons, procedures and tactics. We would be fighting along side our allies in Normandy or later in the Netherlands.

The division adopted a unit code name which was used during the rest of its existence. The 501st Parachute Infantry Regiment was called Klondike. The colors red, white and blue were adopted for the 1st, 2nd and, 3rd battalions. The regimental emblems were suits of playing cards. The 501st was diamonds. Battalions within regiments were identified by marks. A mark on the right side of the emblem on the helmet indicates the first battalion, at the bottom of the emblem, 2nd battalion, at the left of the emblem, 3rd battalion, and at the top of the emblem, headquarters company.[11]

501st Regiment	1st Battalion	Company C
Klondike	Red	Charlie

Diamond (helmet marking)

My helmet markings were on both sides of the helmet just above the ears - a diamond bar. On the back of my helmet I had a horizontal luminous white strip 4 inches long and 2 inches wide identifying me as a non-commissioned officer. All of the other regiments had similar markings as to kind, so it was easy to identify the "friendlies" in the field. Sergeant Guy Sessions and I were sent to another teaching training course for glider pilots for two days to teach them map reading compass use and an orientation to the rifle

---

11 The division adopted unit code names. O'Brien. With Geronimo Across Europe, pge. 88.

company weapons that they would encounter after they landed their gliders in enemy territory. They would go from pilots to infantrymen in an instant and must carry their own load and provide for their own safety, instead of wandering through enemy territory in despair, seeking friendly battle lines. The army evidently had overlooked the salvation of the glider pilots. We needed them for future operations. They were put to guarding German prisoners as long as they stayed with us. Some even took up the rifle and joined us in combat.

While the Chicago/Neptune airborne phase of Operation Overlord was maturing in the spring of 1944, the 501st regiment was participating in a three phase series of coordinated plans that involved more men and materials than the preceding exercise. These exercises were conducted along the English coast in county Devonshire from which 3000 inhabitants had been evacuated. The major seaborne operational area was Slapton Sands for Force U, Force O, and Force B. The three great airborne operations had allowed the commanders and the men to gain needed experience, but it also had the effect of confusing the enemy. The operations caused the Germans to be alerted as their aerial and reconnaissance and intelligence reported massing of invasion-size armadas and to have nothing to happen again and again. For the 501st it resulted in strayed parachute drops for the platoons, snafued communications and jump injuries.[12]

    The 501st took part in three of the ten exercises.
    The first of these was Exercise Beaver.
    Date: March 27 - 30, 1944.
    Place: Southwest corner of England near the port Torquay.
    Geography: A tactical reproduction of Utah Beach in Normandy in that Slapton Sands was along a narrow beach separated from the mainland by a long narrowfresh water lake adjoining a swamp land and crossed by two bridges.
    Objectives: To capture four causeways from the mainland to Utah Beach allow the invasion forces protected passageway into the interior.

---

[12] For the 501st it resulted in strayed parachute drops for the platoons, snafued communications and jump injuries. Ambrose, <u>D-Day, June 6, 1944,</u> pge.136.

Trial by Combat

Jumps: From the tailgates of General motors trucks, GMC), simulated airdrops, assembly of the forces and proceed with the exercise.

The second Exercise was Operation Tiger.
Date: April 23 - 30, 1944.
Place: Southwest corner of England. The same place as Beaver.
Geography: A tactical reproduction of Utah Beach in Normandy, France. The same area as Operation Beaver.
Objectives: To capture four causeways from the mainland of France behind Utah Beach, to allow the invasion forces, Force U, a protected passageway to the interior. After the 501 dropped on plowed fields, it captured a simulated road junction at Ste Marie du Monte, Ste Mere Eglise and two bridge crossings on the Mederet River. The airborne phase was completed by 0300 a.m. The troops began the return trip to Lambourne by train.[13] This correspond to the Neptune Phase of Operation Overlord jumps: Air landings were simulated as in Operation Beaver. We were brought up to the drop zones ahead of time, in trucks, and jumped from the tailgates.

The third and final dress rehearsal was Exercise Eagle. This exercise was named by General Maxwell Taylor, our division commander, 101st Airborne Division.
Date: May 9 -12, 1944.
Place: To be held inland in the nearby Wilts area north of Newbury and Hungerford. The 501 Parachute Infantry Regiment moved by train to Merryfield airport marshaling area. The same C-47's were to be used that were assigned in the two previous exercises, Beaver and Eagle.
Geography: Same as exercises Beaver and Eagle.
Objectives : Capture and clear four Normandy beach causeways leading inland from a simulated Utah Beach, to secure all flank objectives and destroy an enemy gun battery W X Y Z covering Utah

---

[13] The Airborne phase was completed by 0030 A.M. and the troops began to return to Lambourne by train, Rapport & Northwood, Rendeezvous With Drestiney, pge. 62.

Beach with its fire power, plus all objectives practiced in Operations Beaver and Tiger.

Jumps: 501st, 502 nd, 506 th regiments were airborne just before midnight of May 12, 1944. The jump started at 2400 on May 11, 1944, and three hours later 75% of the personnel and 90% of the jettisoned equipment bundles were gathered.

Numerous tactical pilot errors again, of the same nature- aoccurred on the two previous exercises. Twenty-eight planes brought back 528 parachutists to their departure airports. Four hundred men were treated for broken bones, sprained ankles, and other jump injuries. Company C had three injuries. Sergeant A. Kromholtz came down between power lines and cut his throat. He dangled above the ground and couldn't extricate himself from his harness, without help, which was slow in coming. He was killed later in Holland on September 17, 1944. Lt. Ed Jansen, company continued the assembly-exercise and disguised my injury.

Upon my return to Camp Lambourne, I taped my ankle with athletic tape that I obtained from our platoon medic, and it remained trussed until after the Normandy invasion, by which time it was completely healed.

There was little time left for healing for the three injured jumpers of company C. After the large-scale divisional exercises of March, April, May were concluded, the 501 regiment held continuous training programs, both day and night, attacking enemy gun positions demolishing bridges and clearing causeways. Every time we went out on an exercise we were issued K rations for three days, gas masks, and of course our weapons plus a mussette bag for all of our personal items. This was the standard procedure for exercises Beaver, Tiger, and Eagle. All equipment parapacks were practiced rolled and the aircraft was loaded for each exercise at Merryfield airport. We assumed until live ammunition was issued it was another dry run. The day we packed rifle ammunition, hand grenades, smoke grenades, phosphorous grenades, 45 caliber machine gun/ gun belted ammunition, metal click- clack recognition implements, we knew it was the real thing. The invasion-date, time and location-lay straight ahead; France.

Trial by Combat

A week before D-day, the officers of company C learned their flight plans and flight pattern from Merryfield airport to upper Normandy (Cotentan Peninsula), France briefings continued down through the company commander, the platoon leader, the squad leader and the last private. The commanding officer of company C, 501 PIR, Captain Robert H. Phillips, describes the painstaking preparation:

Several days were devoted by the unit commanders, of which I was one, to study our assignments and formulate detailed plans for carrying them out. Each individual company officer was thoroughly briefed on the detailed plans of his particular unit - the company. Only general information was given as to the mission of the 101 st Airborne Division. My company C's mission was to seize and secure the road junction south of Ste. Come de Monte, a small village, thus securing the flank of the drop zone (DZ) D. This position also overlooked the main highway bridge north of Carentan, and later gained the name of "Dead Man's Corner"

As the days and hours passed, each company was prepped with additional invasion information regarding their missions. Company C was to parachute on drop zone D (red) preceded by three flights of pathfinders (12:42 A.M.). Drop zone D was about 1728 yards long and about 500 yards wide, cross-hatched with hedgerows and canals about 6 feet wide and 7 feet deep, which created irregular shaped fields. We were now aware of some of our responsibilities before the invasion but more was to come after we were confined to Merryfield airport marshaling area.

The days and nights for invasion preparation were over in the Lambourne fields. The 501st was put on 'red alert' by the end of May, for several days. We could not leave the compound area of our quarters or talk to any civilians, which included all English citizens of Lambourne. Guards were posted at all perimeter hot spots and the gates were locked. We would be moving out again to the Merryfield airport at any moment. The supply sergeant violated the confinement order by talking to an English girl, who came to the gate, peered through a slot and asked for the supply sergeant. He answered the call and was summarily arrested and confined until the company boarded the aircraft for the invasion. He was killed several days after he landed in Normandy. This was only the beginning of a sordid story a tabloid court case which was really never resolved.

By the first of June we were trucked to the same airport and marshaling area for the fourth time-Merryfield. The citizens of Lambourne in the shops and the streets waved good by as we passed along their streets so familiar to us. Their foreheads were etched with a valley of sorrows. They seemed to feel that something was different this time.[14]

I am sure that these ideas of the invasion were in their thoughts for they had witnessed this three times: by our training, by our intellectual declaration, by their emotional expressions we would sink our eagles talons deep in the soil of France. We were airborne and we were the sharpest point of the technological sword of the invasion. The citizens of Lambourne knew that Operation Overlord would be no spring reverie for the 501st. Their most formidable thought might be that the Germans didn't build a defense made of mud and manure. Even if the Germans did they couldn't put a roof on it. There was always a way in for the 501st; we were coming through the roof by parachute. Finally in the midst of so much sadness and sorrow, there was plenty of warmth and some humor. Men don't go into combat for light and transient reasons but rather for deep philosophical principles. This includes the rank and file of the company.

When the 501st trucked out of Lambourne, England, my thoughts were of Merryfield Airdrome. My thoughts about the army and my training were something like this; the army is like a potter, who works with clay. The ingredients are drawn from the north and the south and as far as the east is from the west. The army, not unlike a potter, squashes, rolls, mixes, and kneads the clay curriculum of the training school until it has a smooth texture, and its consistency is uniform. Thus the army gives us a basic course for survival by fashioning a trail to victory from Camp Toccoa to Camp MacKall.

The army infantry training was the curriculum of the ancient tradition and the art of survival taught by non-professionals. To

---

14 Their foreheads were etched with a valley of sorrows. Finally in the midst of sorrow there was some warmth and humor. They seemed to feel that something was different this time. Rooney, My War, pge.15.

Trial by Combat

the intellectuals, Army instruction was like a morass of century-old swamp grass cultivated with chicken shit. The curriculum was fish-grabbing (judo and martial arts) woolly horse clubbing (camouflage techniques) and saber-tooth tiger scaring (marching firing). This was the extent of our offensive / defensive combat action to be used against an entrenched and seasoned enemy. Another short-fall of our training was "How to control fear." They should have taught us how to accept fear by changing the way we think-change our perception to accomplish our combat objective. The army failed to isolate each of us (on field problems) in order to experience fear.

The Army was like an incubator-it tried to mold us. They are trying to make us killers, as every soldier must be a potential gangster. Remember, we were out to kill: kick them in the balls, hammer their heads, stab them and strangle them with piano wire. Combat, when reduced to its essential elements, is to kill or be killed. What will Axis Sally and Lord Haw Haw say about the 501st Parachute Infantry Regiment. Let Colonel Johnson reaffirm it. Let the invasion begin. We are the key to unlock Hitler's roofless fortress of mud and manure, through the roof we will come.[15] The Earthquake said to Colonel Johnson, " I will shake the earth." The colonel replied, "We will do away with that which can be removed. If we don't succeed, please return. Let the 501st begin the ordeal of destruction." Airborne is the magnificent multiplier of the field commander's prime assets of choice-speed and surprise.

---

15 Let the invasion begin. Op. Cit., pge.6

Chapter 8

The Enemy

Spawn of an accursed race,
Turn and meet me face to face !
Here amid the wreck and rout,
Let us grip and have it out,
Here is where ruins rock and reel,
Let us settle steel to steel !

Robert Service, Rhymes of the
Red Cross Man

As D-day approached we felt confident that we were as well prepared as we could possibly be. We had spent a long time thinking about what we would do when we first hit the ground in enemy territory, but we had given too little thought to what kind of welcome the Germans had prepared for us. For many months Rommel and some of the best military minds in the world had been building defensive positions all along the Atlantic coast from Norway down to Spain. They did not know the exact date of the invasion, nor did they know the exact place where the Allies would land. But they knew the assault was about to take place, and they knew what areas were best suited for amphibious landings. They were also fairly certain that the amphibious attack would be preceded by an airborne invasion. Those areas that would be most vulnerable to amphibious and airborne invasions were especially well fortified. One of these places was the Cherboug/Contentan Peninsula of Normandy, where, of course, the invasion was finally launched.

The Germans had standardized their defensive strategy in all of their occupied territories, and this peninsula was generally set up accordingly, but with additional installations tailored to the particular characteristics of the Normandy landscape.

Defensive points were usually built around three horizontal arching belts of fortified positions. Each belt had specific missions with artillery and tank back-up. The defense systems ranged from seven to ten miles in depth.

The first belt of defense was called Battle Outposts, and began about a quarter of a mile from their front line; in this case their shore line, and stretched about one-half mile in depth. All soldiers were considered expendable in an attack. Their primary purpose was to delay the enemy. All natural terrain features were given paramount fire power attention in establishing strong points such as sunken roads, stone farm houses, rivers and their tributaries, and village streets. Machine guns, mortars and artillery were sighted on obvious approaches.

General Rommel ordered all fields suitable for glider and parachute landings behind the coastal zone to be staked. The stakes (trees) were to be placed close enough together so that gliders could not come down between them. They were topped with Teller mines and wire was strung between the posts (trees). These hellish contraptions were known as Rommel's asparagus. God help any parachutists who landed on them.

Open pastures were mined and laced with barbed wire.

All Battle Outposts were interconnected by a series of maze-like trenches for reinforcing strong points of escape if over-run.

The second belt of defense was known as the Advanced Position, situated about one mile behind the Battle Outposts. All soldiers were ordered to sit tight, defend the ground, and wear down the enemy, then counterattack. They were never to retreat, even if the Battle Outposts were over-run. The Advanced Positions were reinforced by

Trial by Combat

more barbed wire entanglements, extensive mine fields, infantry in depth with interlacing fire, tanks, mobile self-propelled Nebelwerfer guns and mortars.

The third belt of defense was called the Main Position, about three miles behind the Advanced Position. It included the high ground for artillery and mortar observation posts. Here were also specialized heavy equipment and Mark VII tiger tanks. On the Cherboug/Cotentan peninsula the Germans were able to take advantage of the swampy, low-lying land just beyond the beaches. By controlling the flow of the rivers that emptied into the English Channel, they were able to inundate the coastal lowlands and make it extremely difficult for enemy troops to move inland if they were somehow able to reach the well fortified beaches.[1]

The German defenses of this peninsula were formidable indeed. The flooded areas would not only be an obstacle to those troops landing on the coast, they would also be a death trap for any heavily-laden paratroopers who happened to land there in the darkness.

The only way these water barriers could be crossed was by a series of causeways which were protected by extensive artillery positions.

Along the beaches, and in the water approaching the beaches, the Germans had constructed elaborate barriers of steel and concrete connected to deadly mines. Some of these mines were powerful enough to blow a landing boat loaded with soldiers clear out of the water.

On the heights above the beaches many pill boxes, bunkers, and other strong points bristling with heavy guns, were ready to pour fire down on any allied soldiers who managed to reach the beaches alive.

The strong points were very ingeniously constructed. They consisted of barbed wire entanglements, mine fields, intricate networks of trenches, and reinforced concrete walls, some of them five feet thick.

---

[1] By controlling the flow of rivers that entered the English channel They were able to inundate the coastal lowlands. Belfield &Essame, The Battle For Normandy, pgs. 119-121.

Thomas M. Rice

On June 5, 1944, the area of Normandy where the allies were about to land was defended by three German divisions: the 709th Infantry, the 243rd Infantry, and the 91st Air Landing Division, which included the elite 6th Parachute Regiment: a total of approximately 40,000 men. In addition to these army units there were contingents of naval coastal gunners, and thousands of Luftwaffe antiaircraft personnel. This meant that the 18,000 American and British airborne troops who landed in the early hours of D-day would be outnumbered almost three to one until the amphibious troops would be able to break through and relieve them.

One of the crucial places in the German defenses was the lock at La Barquette. This lock on the Douve River was especially important to the hydraulic engineers. Over a period of years, they used the lock to flood the lower pastures (polders) behind the eastern continent peninsula where they believed any amphibious landings were most likely to take place. With the lock closed, the drainage from the Mederet River into the Douve River, from higher northern ground, would create a broad flood plain and inundate the Mederet River channel to its origin. When the lock was closed, by heavy wooden beams, the incoming English Channel tide would cause the Douve River to overflow its banks and, again, flood the polders from the lock eastward to the Escart Estuary.

The area around the lock was defended by the German 6th Parachute Infantry Regiment. This elite unit was under the command of Baron Fredrich von der Heydte. His crack regiment had distinguished itself in the battles at Poland, France, Russia, Crete, and North Africa.

It so happened that one of the major D-day objectives of my outfit, the 501st Parachute Infantry Regiment of the 101st Airborne Division, was to capture, hold, and control the La Barquette lock the night before the American troops stormed Utah Beach. So it was that Colonel Johnson's green, untried Americans would get their first battle test against Baron von Heydte's vaunted German 6th Parachute Regiment. It was to become a clash between two systems: the totalitarian Nazi vs. the freedom-loving Americans. As Fate would have it these two units would meet numerous times in the battles to come, and there would be much killing and dying taking place among them; but in the end the German 6th Parachute Regiment was destroyed and ceased to exist as a fighting unit in Normandy.

On the night of June 5, 1944, as we boarded the planes that would take us into battle, I'm not sure we realized the full extent of the dangers and difficulties we faced, or if we thought about the hundreds of thousands of other men who faced similar or even worse ordeals, but if we had known all this, it would have made no difference to us. We were ready and almost eager to go into action and get the whole bloody thing over with.

Thomas M. Rice

Thomas M. Rice & Frank Carpenter, Company C, 501st Parachute Infantry Regiment, Mourmelon, France, 1944

Trial by Combat

Thomas M. Rice, Camp Lucky Strike, Nice France, homeward bound

Thomas M. Rice

Roster of the 501st Parachute infantry Regiment, 101st Airbourne Division, Company C, Lambourne, England, February, 1944
Row 1 (top row) Fred Henry, Michael Leashak, Kenny Ryan, John Thomas, Paul Sanders, Charles Elder, Stanley Del Santos KIA, Donald Moore, Floyd Martin, Dan Olney, Hillel Rosenthal, George Zebrowski,
Row 2 Adam Canup, Edward Heinze, John Cipolla, John Blicha, Samuel Konochuck, Alvin Hotchkiss KIA, Dominic Spolodiro, David Snowden, (name unknown) Joseph Schwarmerberg, George Hall KIA, Ed Smith, Francis Beavers
Row 3 Nick Zerille, John Curtis, Adolph Ciummo, Harold Krainer KIA, Gene Acevedo, C.L. Gasper, Arthur Texiera, Jack Welch, Harry Ward, Jack Ertl, Richard Madison, Tony Das, Frank Ficarrota KIA
Row 4 William Hixon KIA, Albert Hutton, James Jacobson, John Armstrong, Charles Chilton KIA, Arnold Kromholtz KIA, Thomas Rice, Paul Mickelson, Myron Sessions, Howard Allen, Louis Rafferty KIA, James Mason, Edward Jansen Ex. O., Robert Phillips, Capt. C Company
Row 5 Gerald Peschka, John Janzen, Walter Myers, Thomas McNabb KIA, Keith Thorpe, Cesidio Ventura, Flora Galus, Thomas Holland

90

Trial by Combat

Row 1: (top row) Fernando Encanino, Floyd Lindley, name unknown, John A. Simmons, name unknown, Robert Hemminger, name unknown, Frank C. Beck, Cornelius Kelly, Sam Sorenson, Floyd W. Wickstrom, name unknown William Fields, unknown, John S. Eyers

Row 2: Amos Casada, name unknown, Paul L. Stafsholt, Howard J. Crossley, name unknown, Edgar Tyron KIA, Peter L. Forte KIA, Robert Harwell, Herbert C. McWilliams, Max Osterman, name unknown, Lonnie Crews, Harold Paulson, Sol D. Bernard

Row 3: John Smith, Robbert J. Kahoun KIA, Duke Day, Elmer Arneson, Richard Cavender, Charles Bowmen, Alvin Henderswon, William Jr. McQuade, Wilford Gray, Geore Gama, Lyle Paulson KIA, Howard C. McClelland, Warren Humma, Milario Compos, Ralph Bradybaugh KIA

Row 4: Charles Bowser, Leo Martin, Marshal Buckridge, William De Huff, Lavern Blend, Norman Engasser KIA, name unknown, Maurice White, Ralph S. De Marco, Donald Kreuger, Leo Beals KIA, William W. House, Larry Kuenzi, Milton Nelson KIA

Sitting: John Pavalesque KIA, name unknown, name unknown, name unknown, Frank Carpenter, Benjamin Jordan, Stanley S. Kolodzeij

91

Thomas M. Rice

Rosenthal, Hillel

Zebrowski, George

Das, Tony

Ficarrota, Frank **KIA**

Thomas M. Rice

The men shown on these two pages are mentioned in this book. Also all these men parachuted behind enemy lines at Normandy, June 6, 1944; six hours before the D-day landings.

Trial by Combat

Kahoun, Robert J. **KIA**

Sessions, Myron

Jansen, Ed. Lt.
Exec. Officer

Phillips, Robert, Capt.
Company C.O.

De Huff, William

Carpenter, Frank

Thomas M. Rice

Captain Robert H. Phillips, 501st Parachute Infantry
Commanding Officer, 1943, extreme left

Trial by Combat

Thomas M. Rice & Marvin Van Buskirk, 501st
Parachute Infantry homeward bound, 1945

Thomas M. Rice

Lt. Eugene D. Brierre, 501st Parachute Infantry, 3rd platoon, Company C

Trial by Combat

Camp Toccoa, GA, Obstacle course, 1942

101st Airborne Division paratroopers boarding aircraft for a practice jump, England, 1944

Parachute Jump Tower, Fort Benning, Georgia, 1942

Parachute Training Tower, Fort Benning, GA, 1943, 250 feet

Trial by Combat

Camp Toccoa, GA, Regimental Area, Mess Halls and Company Quarters, circa 1942

Camp Toccoa, GA, Training area, rifle range, Aircraft fuselage, 1942

Thomas M. Rice

Camp MacKall, Hoffman, North Carolina,
Advanced Airborne training, 1943

The Johnson Memorial and Johnson Field are in the 2nd Brigade area at Fort Campbell. Colonel Howard R. Johnson, the first commander of the 501st Parachute Infantry Regiment was killed in action in Holland. (photo by Paladin)

The Screaming Eagle, November-December 1990

Colonel Howard R. Johnson Memorial Grave Marker, Fort Campbell, GA, Commanding 501st Parachute Infantry Regiment

Trial by Combat

S.S. William Geothals, Liberty ship #242579, 501st Parachute Infantry on board bound for England, December 1943

La Barquette Locks, Carentan, France, D-Day objective of 101st Airborne Division, June 6, 1944

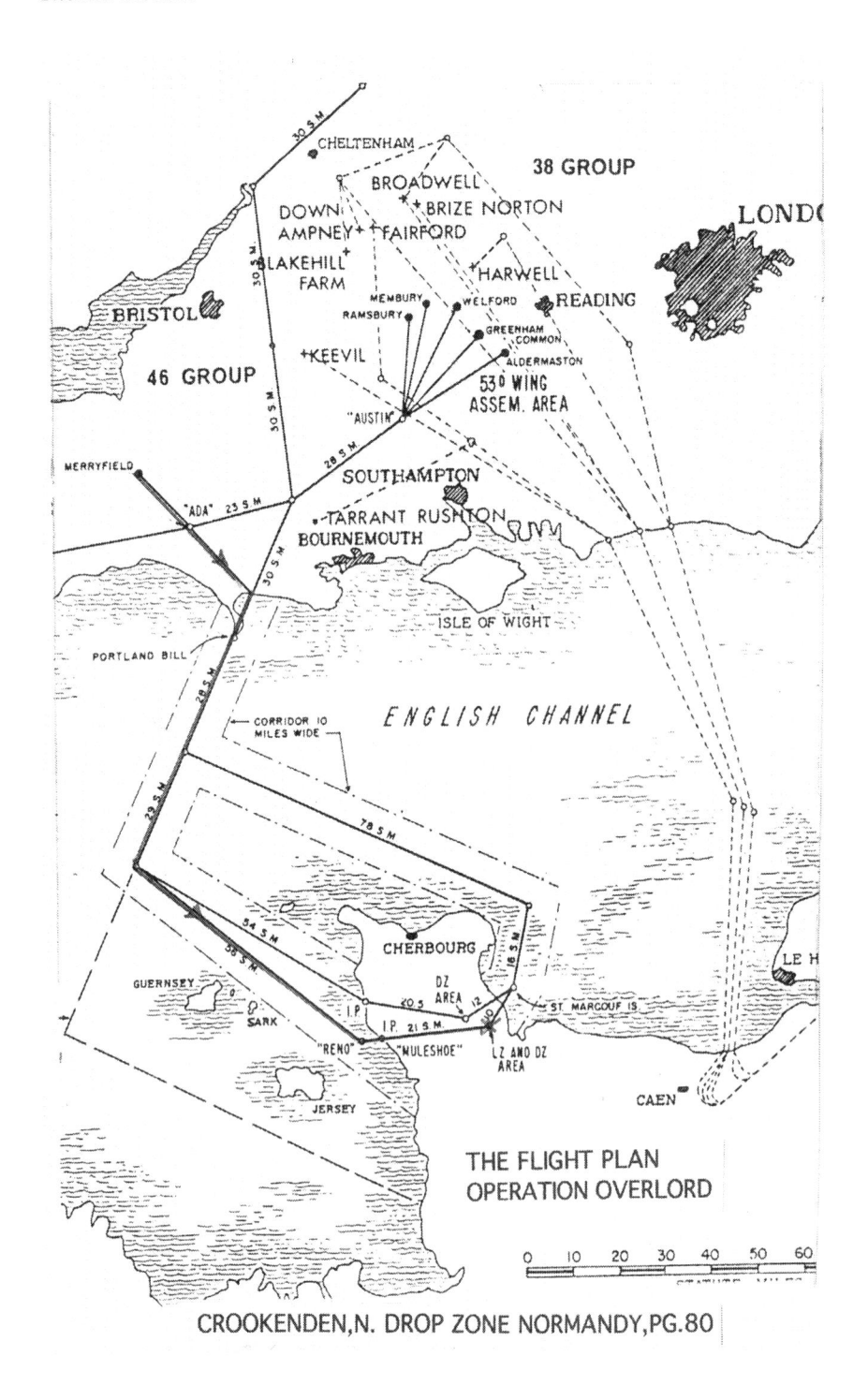

CROOKENDEN, N. DROP ZONE NORMANDY, PG. 80

Trial by Combat

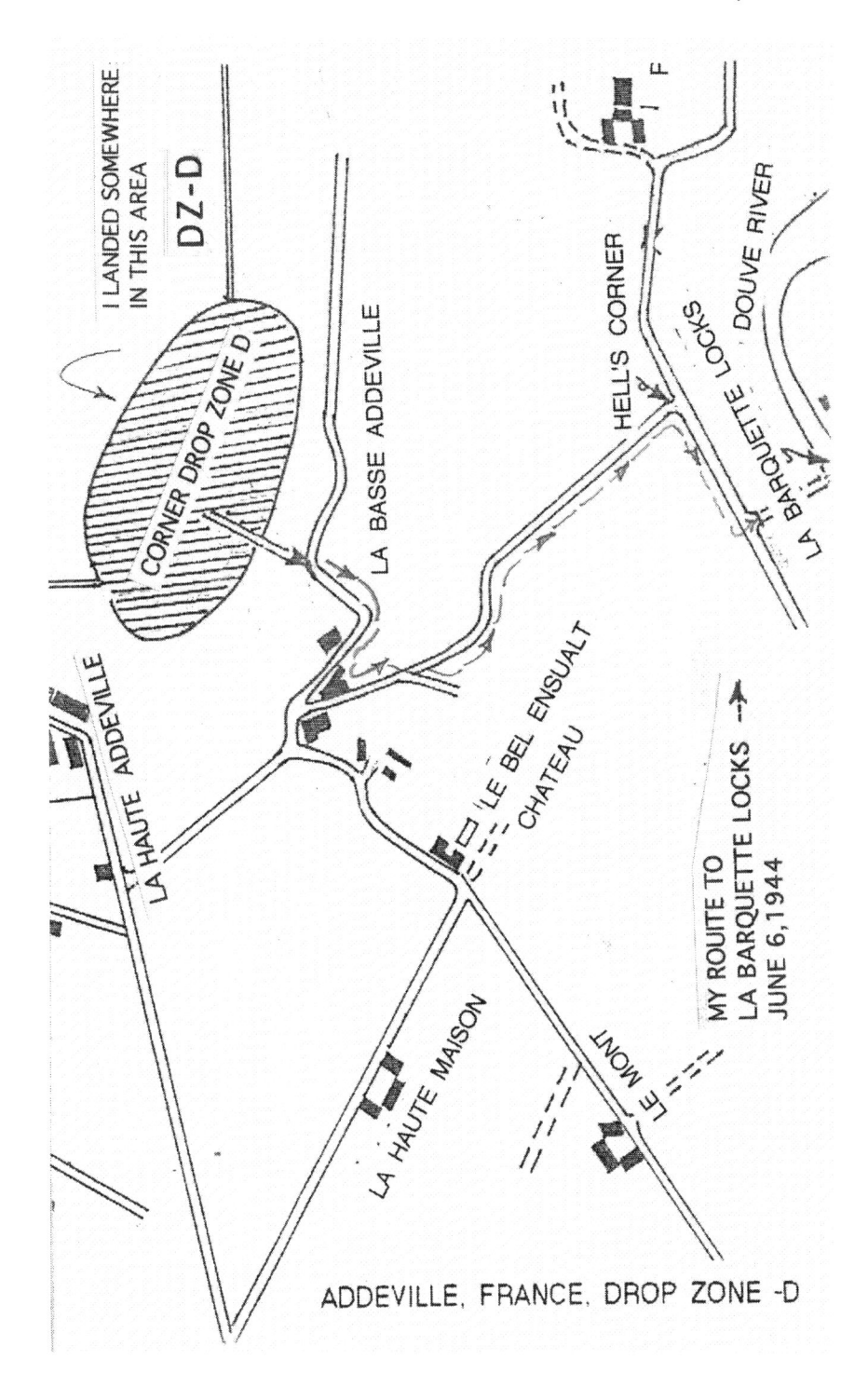

BATTLE AT PENEME-LA BARQUETTE AREA
JUNE 6-7, 1944

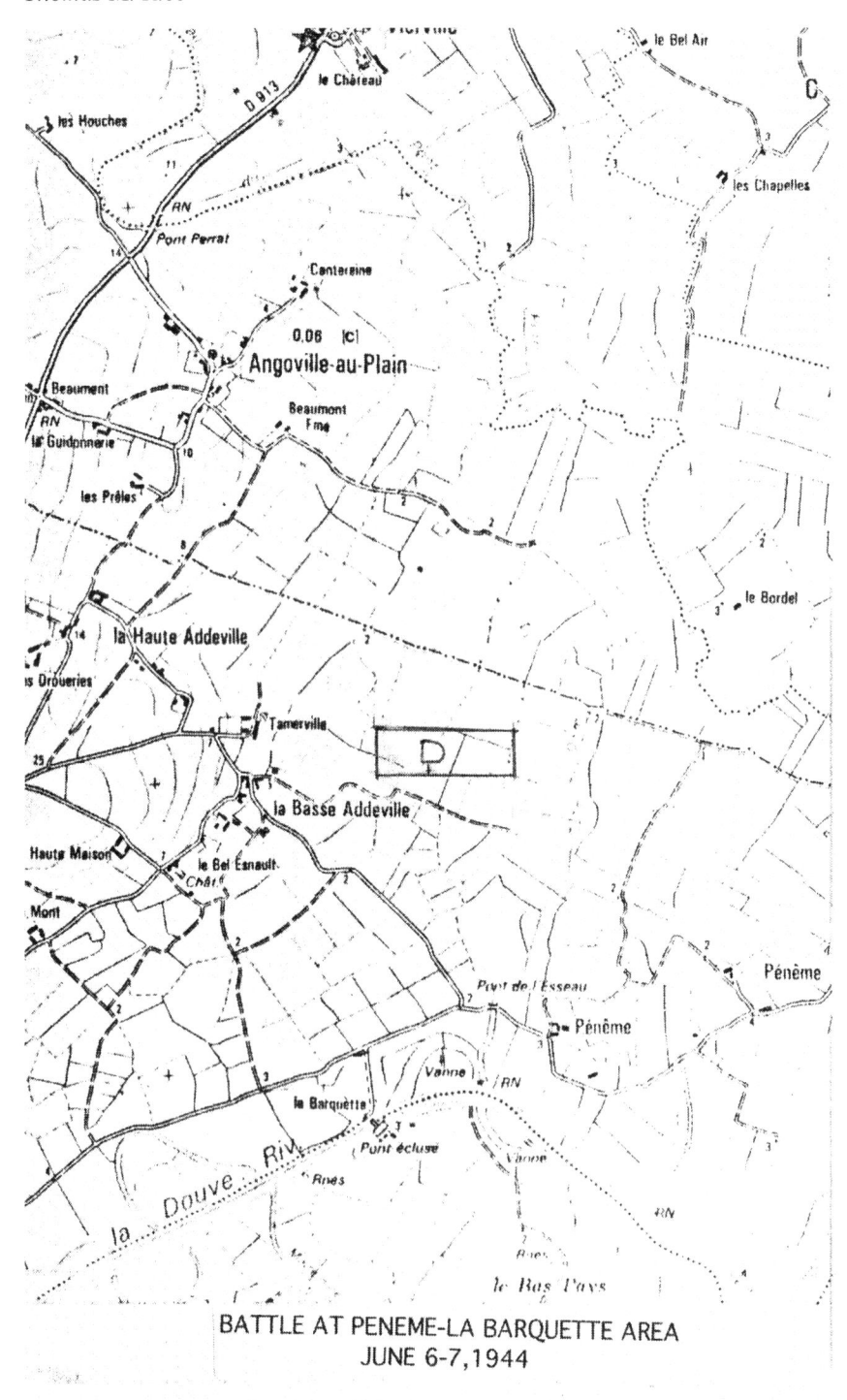

Trial by Combat

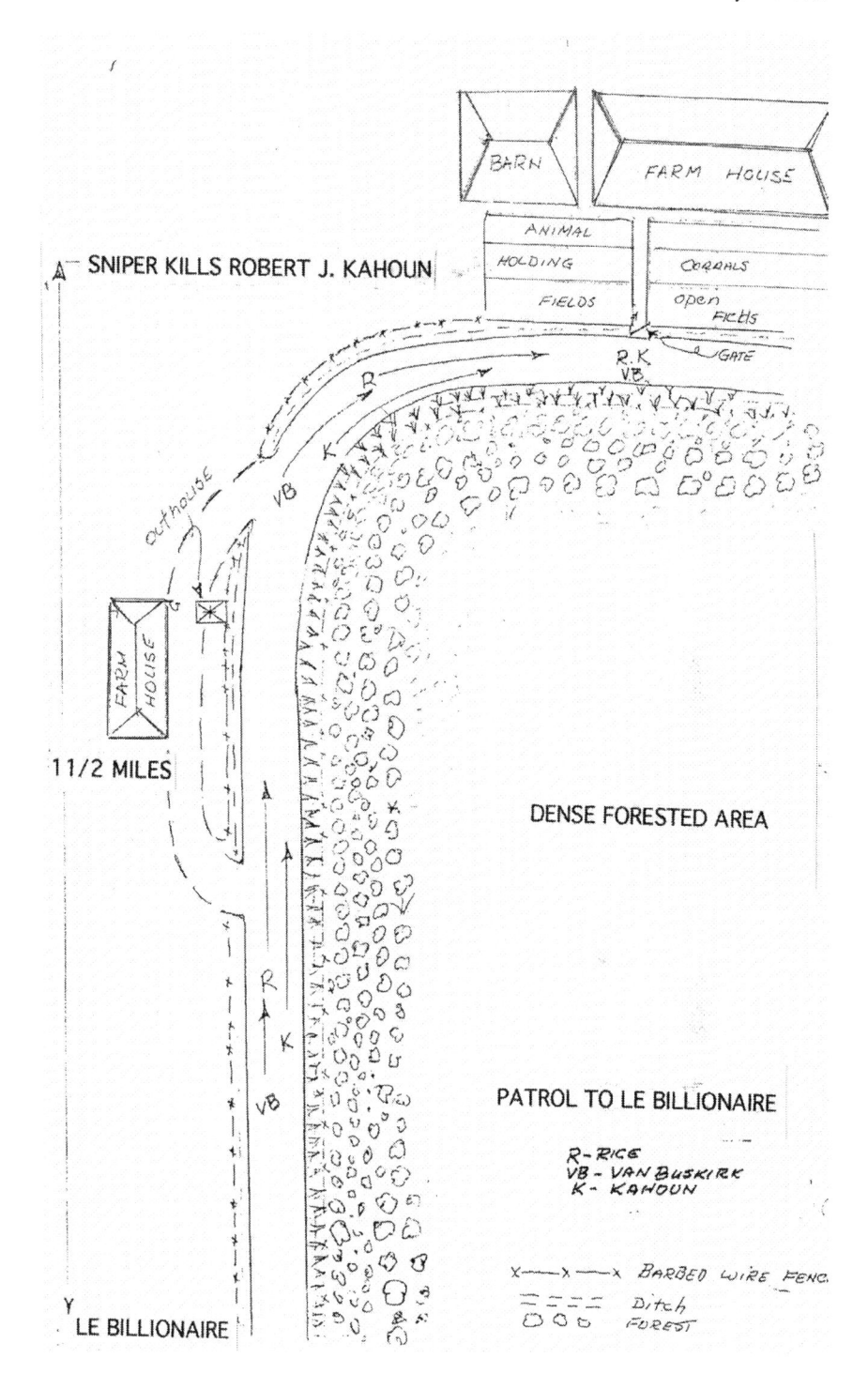

Thomas M. Rice

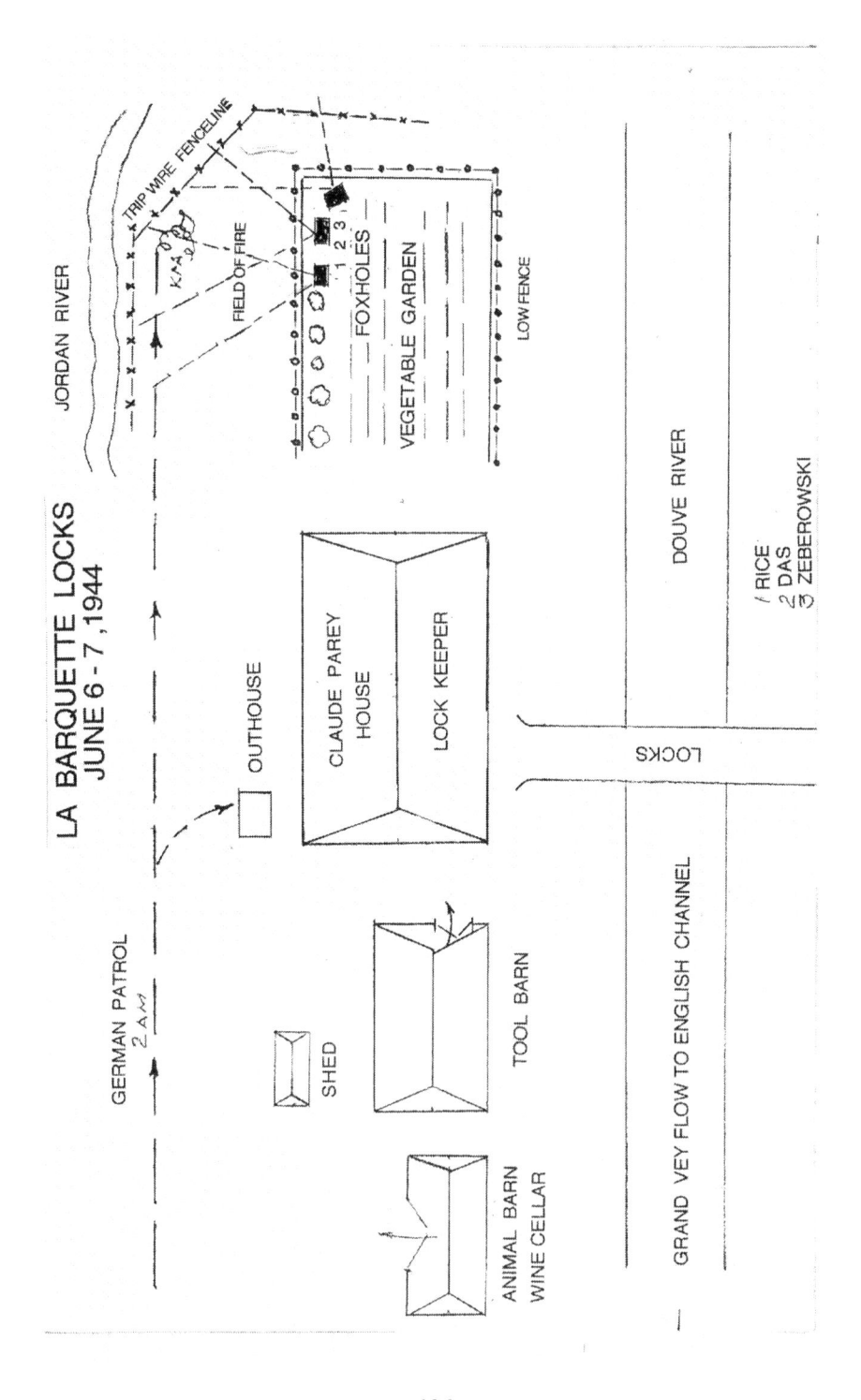

Trial by Combat

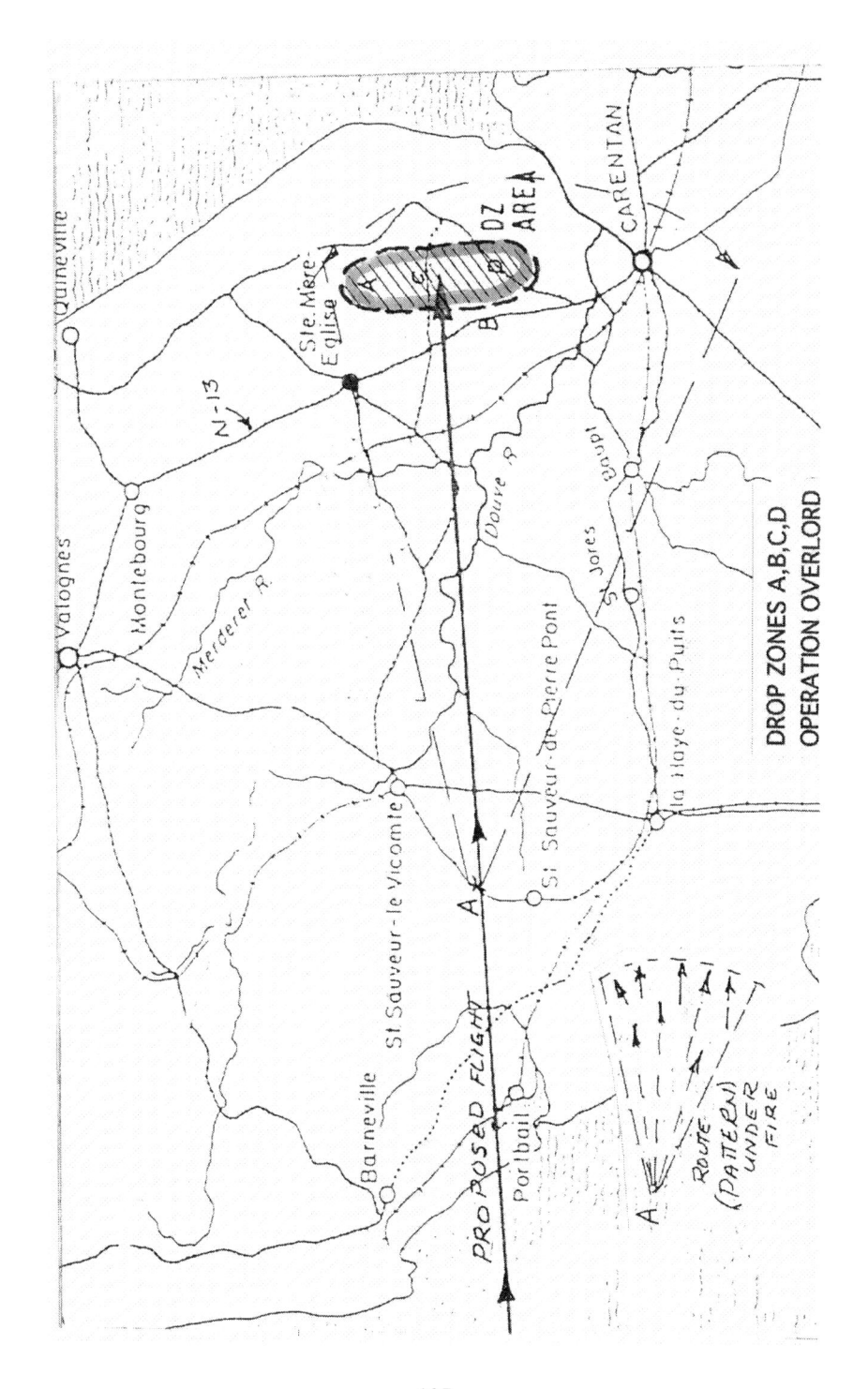

Chapter 9

Cross Channel - Low Angle of Attack

OH YEA WHOSE HEARTS ARE RESONANT,
AND RING TO WAR'S ROMANCE,
HEAR YE THE STORY OF A BOY,
AND THE ALLIED INVASION OF FRANCE
(A PEASANT BOY OF FRANCE)
      ROBERT SERVICE.

  On to Merryfield marshaling area again, for the fourth time, as it is now late May to early June, 1944. The time for casual details is over. No K.P. duty (kitchen patrol) or guard duty. Life is pretty much the same as it was in the field and on the three operation exercises. Most of us knew that in a few days we would be fighting along the Normandy bocage (hedgerows). This is Operation Overlord-the first moment of liberty and freedom for the enslaved European citizens.

  It is a time for waiting with an occasional flurry of activity, movies, baseball, reading, letter writing, cutting each other's hair scalp lock, putting the final touches on personal equipment. Just resting took up time punctuated by cross-company visits and occasional fist-fights. Everyone is jumpy. Company C slept on canvas cots in pyramidal waterproof tents, used "honey bucket" latrines and bathed from steel helmets, again.

Intricate details were worked out for the regiments, battalions, companies, squads battle assignments, on sand - table - mock-ups. Carl Cartlege, P.F.C.an S-2 (intelligence section), 501 Parachute Infantry Regiment, relates the following detailed story of secrecy. He was commissioned a second Lieutenant later.

My section of 6 men are detailed at Hempsted Marshall, to guard the sand tables. There were two sand tables, one in each of two small wooden buildings, with two rolled barbed wire fences surrounding the buildings, with one gate at the end of each building. On one of the sand tables is the 501st areas of Normandy and the one in the second building is of all the beaches, every hedgerow, every house, every road is in place. They all looked like one would see the landscape from about 5000 feet. There are two of us (guards) outside the barbed wire twenty four hours a day for about five days, one at the gate and one at the back, each armed with a submachine gun. Our orders are to stop anyone approaching, and ask them to produce their B.I.G.O.T. card. (only a few officers were identified as having knowledge of the time, place of D-Day.). They were to place it in their right hand, next to their cheek, then advance forward. Their picture is on the card. Any deviation from this, we will capture them or kill them. The front gate at Hampsted Marshal is locked and no one came night or day, until about the fourth day, when a command car drove in, with half-black lights on, and stopped about fifty yards away. I am at the gate and flashed my light on them. There are six people in the the car. The driver stayed seated. General Eisenhower and his aide got out, along with Air Marshal Tedder (British) and his two aides. I halted them, asked them for their B.I.G.O.T. cards and then advanced them forward. General Eisenhower came up first, pressed the B.I.G.O.T card to his cheek, and gave me his famous smile, and so did his aide, of course no salutes were exchanged." Air marshal Tedder nor his aides produced their cards. It was a breach of orders, but I recognized him and opened the gate. General Eisenhower was the last to go in, and as he passed me, clasped his hand on my shoulder and said, "How is it going soldier?" "Just fine, Sir." I answered. But the

Trial by Combat

general knew that Air marshal Tedder had breached the order and that I hadn't made a big deal out of it.[1]

Every combatant from colonel of the regiment to the private in the squad passed through the two small wooden buildings that housed the "B.I.G.O.T ed" battle plans. Each studied and memorized the landmarks and locations of the invasion objectives and finally compared each of the objective to the 3-1 : 100, 000 scale maps that were issued to them. They were the fortunate: I was the unfortunate. I was chosen and assigned to the battalion executive officer, Lt. Col. Robert C. Carroll for twenty hours within the marshaling area I was his personal 'batman.' It is a complex responsibility to be in the possession of secrets, even though intelligence information is often restricted for reasons of rank and national security. The result is that I was unable to have time to see and study the sand-table mock-up in the B.G.O.T.ed buildings., even though I was issued the three small scale maps to fool the Germans, if I was captured. I can tell you now after 50 years +, that no one knew the whole story of D-day. None of the 13, 200 paratroopers who jumped into Normandy that night and the next morning knew a major part too well. Certainly, I didn't. Finally, each of us was issued $10.00 in newly printed crisp French franc notes by the American Banknote Company. Much of it exchanged hands by various gambling games in the marshaling area. We called it "funny money." I still have most of my French franc note issue.

Again, the Merryfield airdrome was a familiar sight to us. We arrived for the last time, for a short stay, going withthe IX Troop Carrier Command, 53rd Troop Carrier wing, 441st Troop Carrier Group, 99th Squadron of serial 14 and 15. They were our chauffeurs to combat. The C-47's were furnished by this command as well as the pilots, co-pilots and crew-chiefs. There was a total of 90 planes for this airlift to France for the 501st regiment. Company C would board, fly, and jump from nine planes of serial #14. I was in plane #3 right side of the lead element. The plane's caulk mark is on the rudder but unknown to me because I gave it little heed during the

---

1 "Just fine, Sir, I answered, but the General knew that Air Marshal Tedder had breached the order and that I hadn't made a big deal of it. Cartlege, <u>Unpublished Manuscript Center of Military History.</u>

111

bustle of flight preparations. I am jumping #1.[2] Marvin Van Buskirk was jumping #18, the last man.

War Department circular #15, dated February 16, 1943, page 6. states: In general, the preparation of private diaries and memoranda will be discouraged and may be prohibited by the theater commander. The writers of diaries frequently keep them in their pockets or in mussette bags where they are liable to be captured by the enemy, thus becoming a source of danger. Sending diaries back home was also prohibited.

Shortly before D- Day, while we were in the marshaling area, verbal orders came down to us from division forbidding all invading troops from taking souvenirs or using a camera. There may have been some written evidence, but if so it was considered low priority. The reason behind the divisional order was obvious. The diary ban was an attempt to prevent the enemy from gaining any information; that was why we were issued three maps. Even if you put them together they didn't make any sense. Only one map was correct for the area. No written records. The ban on souvenirs was to protect any trooper from retaliation should he be captured while in possession of any German items. The ban on cameras encompassed all of the other reasons. Your photos might have been used as evidence that you were an accused war criminal. We can be grateful that a few individuals made the remarkable effort to violate these orders or rules.[3] All of these rules will be hard to enforce in the chaos of combat preparation and military action.

At Merryfield airport, Colonel Howard Johnson, commanding officer of the 501st Parachute Infantry Regiment, about two hours before jump time, June 5, 1944, before his assembled regiment made his famous "knife speech," a talk that he looked forward to since the war began and which he had rehearsed for many months. Our ears were wide open to hear his perceptive message. We looked at him with our domestic (civilian) eyes and put the message in our hearts.

---

2 Company C will board, fly, and jump from nine planes of serial#14. Op Cit pge.67.
3 The ban on souvenirs was to protect any trooper from retaliation should he be captured while in possessions of any German items. Bando, The 101st Airborne Division at Normandy, pge. 7.

112

He moved to a position of sanctity. While standing on the hood of a jeep with his high pitched voice even louder than usual, he exhorted his men to give all in the invasion. Standing before them he yelled,

> I am proud of you; you have shown me what you can do. You have shown yourselves what you can do. I have confidence in you! We have worked together, we have sweated together, trained together and played together. Tomorrow night you will be fighting Germans! Are you ready? What we do tonight will be written in history.

There would be no fruitless deeds in the darkness. The carefully calculated climax to the Colonel's speech emboldened him to raise a trench knife over his head for a dramatic blow and final line. He stooped to release the weapon from the scabbard on his ankle, but for a few embarrassing moments the knife wouldn't yield. Turning red-faced, at this seeming interruption, Johnson removed his Bowie knife from his waist and raised it on high. He poised it dramatically; his voice became a scream, "Ere another dawn, I swear to you before tomorrow night this knife will be planted in the back of the foulest black-hearted Nazis bastard in France.[4] Are you with me?" His faithful minions replied, with a blood curdling roar, "Let's go get 'em! Good hunting" We recognized the spiritual reality of his message. Johnson jumped down from his perch atop the hood of the vibrating jeep, and with his eye to destiny, bounded like a turkey vulture seeking a dead carcass to put on his equipment and make any parachute harness adjustments.

> Once more unto the breaches, dear friends, once more, or close the wall with your English dead! in peace there's nothing so becomes a man, as modest stillness and modesty; but when the blast of war blows in our ears, then imitate the action of a tiger; stiffen the sinews summon up the blood, disguise fair

---

4 " I swear to you before the night is over this knife will be planted in the back of the foulest black-hearted Nazi bastard in France."Ibid, pge.36.

nature with hard favor'd rage; then lend the eye a terrible aspect.

Colonel Johnson's speech and personal touch gave me the strength to face the possibility of being killed. Immediately following His "going to war "speech, and before he got his battle uniform, Colonel Johnson indicated he wanted to shake the hand of every warrior. As we lined up, I could see his inner strength come forward to illuminate and extend God's blessings to each of us as we passed one by one, some of us to eternity. It was at this moment-father and son, he shook my hand meaning, God in you ; God with you. He blessed me with His spoken words. God dwells in me as a Holy Tabernacle. In doing so, he created a blaze of fire to help destroy evil. As I boarded the plane, the battle touch, the battle speech, the battle torch gave me strength to enter his Holy Cathedral. He brought order out of chaos. I put the message into my heart. We don't go as thieves in the night, but we go and they will know we have come. General Eisenhower said, " You will enter the continent of Europe as a coiled spring. Let the light of battle be in your eyes." We will seed the night with jumping men who will be scattered in a wind-swept storm over four hundred square miles in enemy territory and drop like over-ripe pears, not like pollen.[5]

The regiment, after the gesture of good will by the colonel, gingerly and silently dispersed to their tents to don their battle togs and march route step to their assigned aircraft.

Let me give you an idea of what I carried and what I was burdened with in combat. I normally weighed 137 pounds, with the addition of my equipment I weighed 265 pounds. It is with difficulty that I could stand up straight and enter the plane. The parachute leg straps were kept loose until it was time to board the plane, but you had to remember to tighten them before the jump. When things get exciting, you could forget.

My equipment was an unusual encumbrance, for it included an ungodly assortment of potentially lifesaving and death - dealing bric-a -brac.[6] I was wearing several layers of clothing; olive drab underwear, light summer uniform of pants and shirt, woolen pants and

---

5 'We will seed the night with jumping men." Orfalea, Lost Battalion, pge. 92.
6 Death-dealing bric-a-brac. Ibid, p. 141

shirt, mussette bag, gas mask, impregnated jump suit, steel helmet, helmet liner with cupped leather chin strap, Thompson submachine gun (fully loaded with 50 rounds of .45 caliber ammunition), 6 clips of .45 caliber ammunition, 50 rounds each, 2 hand grenades, three maps of the Normandy area scale 1:100, 000 (one inch on the map equals 15.8 miles on the ground), sox, extra underwear, tooth brush, razor, soap, face towel, 1 pound cake of maple sugar (a gift from my girl friend), trench knife, machete, first aid bandages, 3 days supply of K rations, pair of jump boots, yellow Mae West life preserver, main parachute, reserve parachute, canteen with water, other personal toilet articles, complete mess gear. This was my complete outfit plus any extra gear that was needed by the squad. This was strapped to us or placed in a drop bag. "How in the hell am I going to carry all of this stuff?" I asked.

Let me tell you about the K rations. These cartons for survival were issued only to parachute troops, but later proved useful to all combat troops. At first, they were a novelty; dinner was the most edible of the three types of meals. It tasted more like food than a can of vitamin complexes. It was a game to fish out the soybean menu crackers, stick of gum, three chelsea cigarettes, synthetic lemon powder, sugar lumps, candy, and a small can of processed cheese. The whole thing was a bit larger that a cracker jack box. It was an American triumph of ingenuity, but after a few months of eating, the only way to get a variety was to eat the box it came in.[7]

>tis the song and sigh of the hungry.
> "Hard crackers, hard crackers, come again no more, many days have you lingered on our stomachs so sore, Oh hard crackers come again no more."
> A soldier's parody of Stephen Foster's
> Hard Times Come Again No More

On Sunday, June 4, 1944, dinner consisted of steak, green peas, mashed potatoes, white bread, ice cream, coffee-all that a soldier

---

7 "It was an American triumph, Gardiner, Overseas, Oversexed, Over here, pge. 40.

could ask for and more. Afterwards we were exhorted to shower and dress warmly. June 4, 1944, was rainy and overcast with a projected continuation of bad weather for June 6. June 5, 1944, is the night we are to jump. A twenty four hour postponement was ordered by General Eisenhower. We went to bed while behind the scenes, General Eisenhower agonized many hours over the signal "GO" to launch us into France. He was told that, under the present conditions, 80% of the paratroopers would be killed and wounded and 90% of the gliders would be casualties before they reached the ground. He also thought what the beach landings would be like prior to the air drop. After a dramatic pause and in a low voice he spoke only a few words. "Let the order stand." There was nothing dramatic in the way that he made that historical remark. He didn't think in terms of history or destiny. He simply weighed rapidly the factors of the situation. The troops are all set; they will never get the fine edge twice. They are the point of the sword.

A promise made to Stalin of a Second Front was already overdue. Public opinion in Britain and the United States clamored for action. Failure to move right now may mean an indefinite postponement and the consequent danger of a 'leak' which would destroy the commander's tactical surprise. Adding all of these variables, seen and unseen, the risk of delay outweighed the risk of mounting immediate action, even though Normandy had the worst weather pattern in forty years. "All right," Eisenhower said, "We move."[8]

Tension was mounting for the men of the 501st. But we kept a song and a prayer in our hearts. We also knew that our lives were being gambled. Before the parachutists entered the field of fire, it was a touch of divine and human nature by Colonel Johnson, the regimental commander, that gave the men courage and enabled them to give proper use of their weapons and accomplish their objectives. Many of them had scalp-lock haircuts, which the officer's frowned upon. They colored their faces with a mixture of cocoa, linseed oil, ashes of paper, soot from engine exhaust, and burnt cork. It was used prior to this as a form of punishment for being A.W.O.L. They all stood at ease in the presence of the general waiting for

---

8 "All right, we move," Eisenhower said. Critchell, Four Stars of Hell, pge. 36.

Trial by Combat

acknowledgement. Another group of paratroopers, the 502nd PIR, at Memberry airport, displayed a unique variety of haircuts; they stood in a row, bowed their heads, and displayed the word V-I-C-T-O-R-Y. Each trooper had a large letter cut from his hair on the dome of his head.[9]

I think we gave General Eisenhower a clear understanding and assurance that we were a powerful force as he circulated among the parachutists just before take-off. At each aircraft, before take - off, General Eisenhower, standing along the side of the runway, had his four public relations correspondents stand back at a distance. He wanted nothing to interfere with his direct personal relationship with the paratroopers on whom so much depended, and he knew that so many of them would die.

On June 5, 1944, after our shower, after our dinner, after Colonel Johnson's "knife speech," after we donned our battle equipment, we started our leisure walk to the assigned aircraft. P.F.C. Marvin Van Buskirk tells the following episode:

"After dinner I took a shower in a canvas stall as a last rite of a human endeavor to cleanse myself body and soul, before take-off for Normandy. I carried with me four layers of clothing to don after the shower. I hung my dog tags on a 2x4 wooden frame supporting the shower stall. This is my only identification because orders were to carry no others. I suited-up and the last item I put on was my parachute, which weighs about 55 pounds. I left the leg straps unbridled and caught up with the rest of the squad, en route on the runway to the aircraft. The conversation with the other squad members of the same stick was light and frivolous until I stopped and froze in place. I announced in a loud voice, 'I left my dog tags hanging in the shower stall! What do I do?' My squad leader Tom Rice's voice rang out loud and clear. 'Marvin, I don't want you to become an unknown soldier. Get a piece of cloth and some nylon suspension lines and make a pair of dog tags. Print your name on both pieces of cloth and thread them for a necklace.'"

Marvin departed and the squad carried his equipment to the aircraft. He soon returned while the stick was loading the 6 parapack

---

9 "Victory," Bando, The 101st Airborne Division at Normandy, pge. 40.

bundles on the under-belly racks of the aircraft and another two in the cabin aft of the jump door. Each bundle weighed about three hundred pounds and it was a chore to stow them in their proper places. Upon Marvin's return, he announced that he had the best set of comfortable dog tags that human nature could devise, in that they didn't clank when he ran, revealing the peculiar tell-tale American presence. We were all excited and it felt like every movement was slow motion.

 Now that we were assembled at the C-47 aircraft, with its white stripes painted on the fuselage and wings, a short time before take-off, which is scheduled for 10:21 p.m., June 5, 1944, eighteen paratroopers of Company C fitted and adjusted all of their personal equipment. The mood was focused and solemn, as each checked the other jumper. Everything had to be right. We had done this three times before for operations Beaver, Tiger, and Eagle with only minor hitches. This time it is to be perfect. The under-belly parapacks were practiced-jettisoned to check the release mechanism. All was okay. Lt. Jansen was the jump master and was jumping as the last man - # 18. He was responsible for tossing one parapack from the jump door with the aid of the crew chief on the "GO" signal, ahead of me. The second round of air sick pills were mouthed and swallowed, without water before we boarded. Then Lt. Jansen gave us the final instructions as we stood beneath the left wing near the exit door. We boarded in reverse jumping order. Each paratrooper was helped up the ladder by the crew of the C-47 and the jumper behind pushed. We were so overloaded and top-heavy that seating was painful, but it would be only a short ride into the bowels of hell and a waiting enemy.

Chapter 10

The Jump - The Landing Flash - Thunder - Welcome

This story shall the good man teach his son;
And Crispin Crispian shall ne'r go by,
From this day to the ending of the world,
But we in it shall be remember'd ;
We few, we happy few, we band of brothers.
                                William Shakspeare

The flight plan for the air invasion was as follows:

Take-off: 10:21 P.M. English double Summer Time from Merryfield airdrome.

Aircraft: 885 DC-3's or C-47 Dakotas.

Distance from England to center of drop zone in France:136 miles.

Elapsed flying time: pathfinders-54 minutes, paratroopers: 58 minutes, gliders: 72 minutes.

Formation: a V of V's of 45 planes per section to fly across the English Channel at 500 feet to avoid detection, then climb to 1500 feet as they cross the French coast at Barnsville, then slope down to 700 feet for the air drop on DZ-D.

Air speed: 150 miles per hour then slow down to 110 miles per hour for the jump. Steady formation to be held. If the drop zone is missed on the run in, the plane is to return to the coast and drop the paratroopers on drop zone D.

Length of the Armada: 200 miles.

Width of the air armada: 10 miles.

Time interval between sections(45) planes: 6 minutes.

Flight plan: direction of flight: Serials rendezvous at 500 feet over southern England to cross the peninsula of land at Plymouth (Portland Bill code name), fly a little west of south for 57 miles to a marker boat in the English Channel, there make a 90 degree turn the left and fly south of east passing over the islands of Jersey and Guernsey and enter on the French coast at Barnsville, west side of the Cotentan Peninsula. From this point (1500 feet) it is about 25 miles due east to the three 101st Airborne Division drop zones- A, C, D. Jump on the green light.

On the basis of an optimistic long range weather forecast that was expected in the early weeks of June, inclement began to set in.[1]

On June 4, American High Command-SHAEF Headquarters was informed that a rain front over the Normandy assault area was expected to clear in several hours. The winds of 25-31 mph were expected to moderate.

On June 5, the weather would be overcast with light rain and stormy with high winds and a cloud base of 500 feet to zero. Forecasting for more than 24 hours was undependable.

On the evening of June 5, the 15th German Army intercepted the 'B' messages which indicated the invasion would be launched within 48 hours.

It was 2215 hours(10:15 P.M.) English Double Summer Time. precisely the time at which the transport planes of the 101st Airborne Division were taking off from eleven English airdromes.

Unfavorable winds and sea conditions were thought by the 15th German High Command to be too adverse for invasion. This report reduced German alertness.

---

1 "On the basis of an optimistic long range weather forecast." Harrison, Gordon, United States Army in World War II, pgs.275.

Trial by Combat

The sea invasion of ships and crafts were launched through the choppy waters in the English Channel and the airdrome armada assembled for the cross-channel attack. Over 6000 parachutists started dropping on DZ (drop zones) A, C, D, Normandy, precisely at 0015 hours for the Pathfinders after a 65 minute flight and 0119 hours for the first flight of the combat troops, after 72 minutes of flight. I jumped at approximately 0130 from serial #14 on the eastern edge of DZ-D at an altitude of 350 feet.

We were aware that we would be the "point of the sword" and that we would bear the brunt of the opening hours of the coming battle-Operation Neptune. We were also aware airborne suffers the greatest casualties because of the near impossibility of their objectives. We must never forget that our mission is to kill even though being killed. That is what the knife speech meant. I keep thinking no matter what kind of night I am having, the morning will always win.

With the plane loaded and ready for take-off, the pilot revved the engines, checked the magnetos, oil pressure, other instrumentation and controls. All the equipment registered proper readings when the pilot feathered the engines, each making a loud popping cracking noise as if they were back- firing. The plane shook and vibrated every rivet as the prop blast rushed by the fuselage and the open jump door. We never had a door closed in flight, in fact we never had a door. We taxied into position. The runway was in the shape of an arrow and the planes alternated their take-off every ten seconds from the head of the arrow, down its shaft and into the sky. We waited for our turn and roared majestically away. Just before the lift-off, I saw General Eisenhower step forward from his entourage and give a perfect military salute-meaning good luck and God speed.

Lt. Ian Hamilton of B company, 501st in another plane, recalled that he penciled-in a last minute replacement on the jump manifest. This soldier was a boxer and a tough guy. As the C -47 was taxing along the runway for take-off, the replacement intentionally fired his carbine rifle that was in his scabbard. The bullet punctured one of his feet and spent itself out the open door of the moving plane. The aircraft was just picking up more speed for the take-off. Hamilton grabbed the trooper by his harness, slammed him against the bulkhead and bellowed, "This yellow bastard won't get the honor of jumping into battle with you brave men!"[2] With that Hamilton flung the offending trooper out of the moving plane and he thumped and bounced along the runway, to be retrieved by the medics on the ground. Following the Normandy campaign, a Board of Inquiry was convened at Mourmelon le Grand, France, to investigate the incident. After testimony was heard, Lt. Hamilton was ruled justified in his action that day.

It was still light bending into darkness when we took-off but night came as we assembled section #14 over England and it made a final pass over Merryfield airport en route to France. Our C - 47 climbed to 5000 feet and fell in formation as the greater number of the other sections rushed their ascent behind us. Within the aircraft cabin, dark and moody, we sat with distorted faces and struggled into body turns to watch the landscape below fade from view. I looked across the aisle at my buddies. They all looked the same-hunkered down, solitary and introspective. Smoking was optional.

Lt. Jansen gave me many preparatory tasks before the take-off, but several were to be executed during the flight. There must be time for solitude and I made time for solitude. I walked forward to the pilot's cabin and told him that I would seat myself in the passage way and lean against the door. If any problem developed, then open the cabin door and I would fall back and wake up. After the second air sickness pill, I was feeling drowsy. The wild excitement of the previous days of June 1, 2, 3, 4, 5 in the marshaling area had subdued me. I was now dozing in the back seat of my memories and have questions, only a few are deep, penetrating and searching. There I was "corum deo," before the face of God. June 6, 1944, was the first time I considered my own death. When the thought of death did occur to me, was someone else's. It had seemed to me that people get old slowly, lose track of time and feeling and fade away until one night they died in their sleep. It never hurt. They had finished life and were unaware of what they were doing and where they were going. They weren't frightened by the thought of anything again. My chance of being mortally wounded is as good

---

[2] "The yellow bastard won't get the honor to jump with you brave men." Geronimo Newsletter, Winter, 1998.

Trial by Combat

as one in five or six, about as good as Russian roulette, which isn't very good at all.³

I don't recall being afraid as much as being introspective with some foresight. I suppose I felt like an ordinary infantryman before the enemy in full fledged combat. If I were alone, I would run but I couldn't because I felt an obligation to the other soldiers around me who were doing the same thing and having the same feelings. Then I realized that I had the same feelings that any one who has ever fought a war has had. It was a combination of anxiety, annihilation, fear of death, and relentless loss of friends. Christianity in military training helped me to face the music even though the tune (combat) was sour.

Fifty Junes later and in recent years, because I am resigned to it, inevitably, I think of death frequently but with less terror and a more thoughtful consideration for what it will mean to family and friends I leave behind. It seems that their lives will be different or better because of my worthy and timely death.⁴

There have been a handful of days since the beginning of time in which the direction of the world has been changed for the better in one twenty-four hour period by the acts of men, June 6, 1944, was one of those days, and for the entire plane load with jumpers.

What the Americans, British and Canadians are trying to do is to get back a whole continent that has been wrested from its rightful owners and whose citizens have been held captive or murdered en mass by Adolph Hitler's German army. It was one of the most monumental unselfish things that one group of people did for another. As it was war that brought the 101st and 82nd Airborne divisions as far as 4000 miles to Britain, so it will be only victory that will take them home again. Their way home has to be fought across Europe by vertical envelopment- the parachute. By the time a week had passed, there would be new place names resonant of Americans in battle. A seven thousand yard crescent-shaped stretch of France's Normandy coastline to be known for generations. History is being made and it will never fall off of the TV screen.

---

3 "My chance of being mortally wounded is as good as one in six", Rooney, My War, pge. 121.
4 "Fifty Junes later and in recent years."Ibid, pge. 123.

The policies of war have to be hammered out by the politicians, the strategy by the military commanders, the reality of war have to be forged by the men of the 101 st Airborne Division-the rifle companies.[5] The flight of section #14 went smoothly across the channel, and after we passed west of Jersey and Guernsey Islands and before we crossed the French coast at Barnsville, we were ready to jump. The red light above the door, which meant five minutes to jump time, glowed in the darkened aircraft cabin. The K ration bundle was in the door, all jumpers were closed up tight, and a second bundle was in line to be tossed out end over end. When section # 14 approached the west side of the peninsula just above Barnsville, low hanging clouds became the major cause for possible collisions as the aircraft were flying tight formations, about one hundred feet between wing tips and staggered to a slightly higher elevation.. The pilots opened up their formations, against military orders, and veered in wheel spoke directions. In the corridor of death, the fog was as thick as my neck. The earth seemed to break open. A hurricane of iron and fire came up to meet us from enemy positions with a deafening roar.[6] The German anti - aircraft batteries, which were to be neutralized earlier but weren't, began to open up and pound our aircraft as we sloped down to jump altitude. What I saw was a pyrotechnic skyline that resembled a fortress with exploding pillars of fire. It stretched far beyond me. I knew we were about to fly into it and through it. I caught only the nearness of a brilliant colorful flame as the heat blasted our aircraft. We were now within the killing zone. As the formation of section # 14 broke up, the pilot began to take erratic flight action, rising and falling with full engine power, twisting and turning to avoid German 88 mm ack-ack which was exploding about thirty feet aft of the tail section. This made standing in the passage way very difficult as the men swayed back and forth and caused them to lose their balance which would make an exit very difficult. We had descended below the planned jump altitude of seven hundred feet to avoid other aircraft but engaged machine gun fire led by red tracer bullets which were striking the wing and

---

5 "Reality of war had to be forged by the rifle companies." Op Cit, pge.149.
6 The earth seemed to break open. A hurricane of fire and iron came up to meet us from enemy positions with a deafening roar. Orfalea, Lost Battalion, pge. 198.

Trial by Combat

tearing metal parts away. The gas tanks were not self-sealing, and if punctured, we would burst into flames. The machine gun bullets sounded like a chain striking metal. I have the fear of being castrated by a flak burst or long traced burst of machine gun fire underneath the aircraft. Looking out the jump door I could see a C-47 engulfed in flames and flying in an arc into the ground. No jumpers exited the flaming plane. It is possible to be so enthralled by some spectacle of war that you are momentarily distracted / captivated away from your own danger at hand.[7] I realize that it is impossible to reduce this extreme danger to an inconvience and still survive.

 We all have days and night in our lives that stand out from the blurr of the days gone by. The night I jump from a C 47 aircraft, bound for enemy territory in France and into the bowels of hell is one of them. The curtain of Roman candle machine gun fire that I went through is another one. It was the beginning of the season of unimaginable suffering and it got worse with each parachute operation. The immediate thought that ran through my mind was that if we didn't get our weapon bundle we would be short of everything but Germans.

 Lt. Jansen tried to calm us as we compressed the line of eighteen jumpers. My nerves were like raw meat hanging in the butcher shop window. Lt Jansen called the pilot on the intercom and asked / told him to slow this craft down to jump speed because we were traveling at 165 mile per hour. "We can't jump at this speed," he said. The pilot refused and the evasive action continued and became more pronounced. The red and white lights, above the jump door, about the size of a fifty cent piece, went out and the green jump light glowed bright. We were over drop zone B which was inundated with seasonial water. The K ration bundle was kicked out of the door by Lt Jansen and the crew chief. I was balancing the second bundle on its end ready to shift it to the door for a drop. As Lt. Jansen and I positioned it in the door, a 20 mm flak burst came in the door and hit the bundle. The explosion knocked me across to the opposite side of the plane. After recovering, without injury, the disgorging

---

[7] It is possible to so enthralled by some spectacle of war that youare momentarily distracted / captivated away from your own danger at hand. Rooney, My War, p. 123

of the second bundle was completed in about forty seconds. This action carried us beyond drop zone B. The plane was still taking evasive maneuvers. The left wing was slowly rising and the right wing was dropping which made the bundle remains untenable. Once the bundle fragments were upright and back in the door, what there was left of it, #2 man Frank Ficarrota and #3 man Tony Das, each at the same time, turned on an electrical switch and a toggle was pulled to jettison the six parapacks under the belly of the plane. The plane rose about fifty feet. The bundles weighing 1800 pounds, fell away from the plane. I followed the shattered second bundle out of the door as the plane rose again. The prop blast threw me against the outside of the fuselage and my left arm, at the arm pit, got caught in the lower left - hand corner of the jump door at the floor. I was hanging on the outside of the aircraft as #'s 2 and 3 jumpers went out the door over me. As the plane dipped and rose, I felt myself banging against the fuselage. My helmet was over my eyes, my legs were almost up to the reserve parachute and bent. I remained in that position for three or four seconds, after which I pushed the helmet up and straightened my legs. I saw the tail of the airplane and the static lines of the other two or three jumpers flapping against the tail section. Upon the next swing into the fuselage, I twisted my body and straightened my arm, which allowed me to clear the aircraft. As the release was taking place, I was scraped from arm pit to wrist and my new Hamilton wristwatch was ripped off. As I fell away, in bad body position, I had a curious feeling of weightlessness. The parachute opened at about 350 feet with a terrible jerk, which tightened all the parts of the harness. The air was rough and dense which caused me to oscillate rather severely-right to left. I was unable to correct this by making riser adjustments to make the best landing possible. I couldn't see a thing. At this moment it was black all around. The only visibility was between shades of black. I hit the ground rolling sideways. The parachute remained inflated and I was dragged toward a field canal. I collapsed the parachute and tried to release both harness buckles to no avail. This wasn't possible because of the extra equipment and the opening shock. I took out my switch blade knife from the double zippered pocket under my chin as I lay on the ground, and began to saw through the risers. They were so thick and heavy duty, by the

Trial by Combat

time I had cut through one-half, #2 and #3 men (Frank Ficarotta and Tony Das) came upon me and helped me to freedom. Believe me, I was glad to see both of them! Good old Ficarotta! I briefly thought back to the time during the Tennessee maneuvers when Frank and I were both disciplined for losing parts of our mortar.

Now, as I think back on those moments after I landed, I have some odd memories. In the few seconds it took me to begin focusing on the awesome tasks that faced us, I thought of how relieved I was to still be alive, and I became very hungry. I wanted to feast, and there were Frank and Tony to help me enjoy the food and drink. Then I wanted to go back to my comfortable habits and define who I was and live out my purpose-to live in freedom before I lose my identity by placing my energy in the proper place influenced by many voices. Let my memory wounds heal.

Then my brain kicked into high gear. Frank and Tony had found our mortar bundle and we distributed the load for easy carrying. The rest of our mortar squad had been scattered widely. Number 18 man, Marvin Buskirk, the man with the home-made dog tags, had landed in the English Channel about 150 yards off shore. Barely able to stay on the surface of the choppy water, and bobbing up and down to gasp for short breaths of air, he was able to discard his equipment before the wind-blown parachute pulled him further out into the channel. His struggle to get ashore was successful only because he was a superbly conditioned athlete-a strong boxer. Within ten minutes of making it to shore he was wounded, but managed to survive, and ten days later he was fighting alongside the rest of us for the capture of Carentan.

As Frank, Tony, and I moved out into the darkness, we were filled with fear. But it was a special kind of fear-not the terror an antelope might feel as a pack of wild dogs closed in on him. We were men, not animals: we were trained for fight, not flight. Our fear was more like that which a tiger might experience as he prepared to attack a grizzly bear. We knew we were in for a very bloody battle. I decided to head east, in the direction of the flight, in order to gather as many men of our squad as possible.

As we groped our way through the darkness we could see in the distance the flashes of the anti-aircraft guns and hear the thunder of their deadly explosions.

Chapter 11

Drop Zone - D Addeville, France

Lead on oh king eternal, the day of marching has come, Henceforth in fields of conquest thy tents shall be our home: Through days of preparation thy grace has made us strong, And now oh King eternal we lift our battle song.
Henry Thomas Smart,
Presbyterian Hymn Book

Frank, Tony and I made our way silently across the sodden pasture, but we were momentarily halted by an irrigation canal perpendicular to our route of travel. Tony Das said, "We're trapped?" We scouted the course of the canal and found no place where it narrowed. Each with a shouldered mortar part, tried to jump the canal which was about eight feet wide and six feet deep with sloping mud banks. I ran and jumped, mindful of all the dangling combat equipment, one foot sank into the mud on the opposite bank as I fell forward to the green sod. Frank Ficarrota's jump wasn't long and strong enough and he landed in the center of the canal with the mortar base plate plus his combat equipment. He sank to the bottom and both of his feet stuck in the mud. He didn't surface immediately. He had to be rescued by hand. He forgot where he was and filled the air with sulfuric fumes of swear words. Tony Das tossed the remaining mortar parts to each of us and he made his jump with success. Frank Ficarrota was drenched and smelled like a cow barn. This commotion attracted the attention of four others who were from our plane and out of sight on a decomposed granite road. They froze in their tracks and clicked their cricket. The pass words and countersign - flash - thunder - welcome were recognized. Our first link-up was made without a casualty. The seven of us didn't know where we were but at least we were safe at that moment. It was 1:50 A.M., June 6, 1944.

As we moved down the road, we hoped toward Addeville, another small group of paratrooper infantrymen, coming up from behind, joined our group in a gesture of good will and support. It was another stroke of good luck. We recognized them as being from our plane by their voices but not by name. Their leader came to me pondering what to do with a hand grenade with a safety pin that had been pulled and dropped (lost). If he had let go of the handle (spoon), at the count of five seconds there would have been an explosion. Even if he had the safety pin it would be impossible to replace it in the grenade as a safety device. I asked him to give it to me and we exchanged the live grenade with caution. I had all the men lie down on the road while I rolled over to the roadside canal and dropped the grenade to the bottom and rolled back as quickly as possible. I counted out loud but softly, the grenade exploded in five seconds spewing water, mud and slime over many of us. Frank Ficarrota was still screaming about his soaked condition and slime on his face. *The war was on!*

The pure fear of the first night-day experience in the pastures of death was like emptying oneself, a complete draining. Another personal thought was that I could be more cruel than I thought I was. There is something forlorn about it Your soul is switched to kill.[1] Killing is and can be clean. An enemy is an enemy and as long as you can believe that you can kill. You shoot to kill. But torture

---

1 There is something forlorn about it. Your soul is switched to kill. Orfalea, <u>Lost Battalion,</u> pge.15-16.

Trial by Combat

is dirty; torture is ugly, foul, twisted, debasing the victim and the wielder of the whip.[2]

Quietly, we formed a patrol looking for trouble or trying to make trouble. We moved out in squad formation down the granite road to Addeville. I saw a French farmhouse about 100 yards off the road on the right side. We must try out what we have learned during the last 1 1/2 years training. I ordered the house to be surrounded in case there were Germans inside to either capture or kill them. They blocked our route to the assembly area. We were told to take no prisoners. I sent Floyd Martin to the front door to knock and act like a civilized human. He was backed by strong fire power in case he got in trouble. Instead of knocking he pounded on the door several times with the butt of his rifle sending sounds rippling across the meadow. A few moments later a French farmer appeared at the door clothed in a long white nightgown which fell to the floor. He wore a tasseled white nightcap, and in his hand was a dish with a lighted candle. It was the essence of a Charles Dickens play. I pushed him aside, since he didn't speak English, as a safety factor, in order to take by surprise any sleeping German soldiers. None were found. We spread a map on the floor and the five of us tried to get the farmer to tell where we were. After much gesturing, he recognized the name of the city of Carentan in the dim light of the house. By his estimate, Carentan was about four kilometers to the south. While this orientation was taking place, the farmer's wife entered from the bedroom in a white nightgown that fell to the floor and her face etched with fright. She was wearing a white nightcap and her candle was flickering in her outstretched hand. She said nothing, but her chief concern was for her husband. We assured them that we wouldn't harm them by crude sign language and we would leave immediately. They recognized our American flag shoulder patch. In a gesture of good will and an attempt to show their support, they gave us the last of their remaining bullets, saving only two for themselves. The rest of the bullets were to be used on the Germans.

---

2 Killing is clean. Torture is dirty. Torture is ugly, foul, twisted, debasing both the victim and the weilder of the whip. Gantter, <u>Roll Me Over in the Clover,</u> pge.130.

Now we had an idea where we were as the first light of dawn began to outline the landscape and define the weather. No enemy in sight. Three of us scouted what we thought was a German strong point by crossing a field and walking by the side of a wounded horse. We found no enemy, so we directed our attention to the horse. His lip was cruelly torn and bleeding from a shrapnel wound, so the medic, Robert Schill practiced a little military medicine and bandage the wounds. The horse snorted shaking his head and trotted a distance trying to remove the bandage. We used the horse as a shield to work our way to safety. The patrol continued along the roadway toward Addeville as a unit, but soon formed into pairs to scout out the roadside houses. As I entered the outskirts of Addeville, which was only a smattering of homes and four streets bounded by ditches, hedgerows and high thick ancient stone walls, a lieutenant from the 326th Airborne Engineer was standing at a gate entrance to a pasture, not unlike the one where I landed. He called to me, "Hey sergeant, get over here!" He gave me an order, "Walk around the perimeter of the pasture and draw some fire from any lurking German sniper." He is telling me to make a trip to heaven just like the ascension of Jesus, himself.[3] The officer assured me that he would stay and cover me on my journey. His objective was to shoot a German sniper and I was the bait. The perimeter of the field was about 600 yards and with alternate bravado and caution I circumnavigated the field without becoming a casualty. When I returned to my point of origin, I expected to see the lieutenant there to give me a report on what he did or didn't see; instead he was nowhere to be found-gone. I was left contemplating his cowardice and decided that I had learned several combat-wise tactics. Never return to your point of origin, exit elsewhere, for you may have been under observation only at the spot where you began. The next conclusion was about my responsibility to stay alive and survive. You cannot win by a stupid sacrifice. You make the enemy take and make the sacrifice. The last conclusion was that there was no state of confusion or panic. His battle order was not a good plan. He was a coward and was going

---

3 He is telling me to take a trip to Heaven jusy like the ascension of Jesus. <u>Ibid,</u> pge. 239-240.

Trial by Combat

to get those in his command killed. A soldier will not willingly and enthustically follow those of rank or title except those who show courage and consideration for the well-being of their men. Never invite ambush by repeating the same patrol along the same route. This is a violation of an elementary infantry principle. Faith in a platoon leader is searching his soul far beyond that which is seen and on display-everyday under garrison life and under combat conditions. I wouldn't hunt with that dog. I wouldn't fight with that dog.

> I am His Majesty dog at Kew
> Pray tell me, sir, Whose dog are you?
> Alexander Pope

I had just found someone possibly more foolish than me. I remained loyal to the royalty of his rank, but the sword of his mouth and the bullets from his eyes indicated he had a hidden agenda, a fire of misunderstanding that diminished the reflection of the silver bars (insignia of rank) on his collar and helmet. His order didn't instill in me ethics. He may have recruited me for his utmost energies as I opened the gate of Hell and entered the killing field-The Pastures of Death.

The Germans believed that a sniper who killed an American in a party of advancing American troops could, when cut off from his escape route, drop from a tree or his hiding place with his hands up in the air and receive the honors of war; but we didn't see it that way and would shoot him. If a Heinie began to holler after his hands were raised in surrender we would give him the works; he would be trying to warn the others. This virtually condemned any German who spoke as he came forward to surrender. We accepted surrender in other unusual ways.[4]

I had passed the first test for survival, but there were many more to come, some of which were narrow escapes. The longer the war continued, the greater the chance I would become a casualty, in one or all of the three categories: disease -a non-battle field injury; wounded in action; or S.I.W, self- inflicted wound.[5]

---

4 If a Heinie began to holler after his hands were up. Kennett, G I The American Soldier, pge.160.
5 "S. I. W. - self inflicted wounds, one bullet in one was fatal. Ibid, pge.175.

Normandy now appears to be a crash course in land warfare, cops and robbers style, even cowboys and Indians. We never knew when one of us was going to get it.

First Sergeant Marshal Buckridge had just called me forward for instructions because we were very low on ammunition and unable to sustain extended combat. I told him that I would get the ammunition but he said, "No you don't, get a volunteer."

I returned to the squad by crawling in the hedgerow ditch and asked for squad volunteers. Frank Ficarrota, after a long silence, was the first to grasp the seriousness of the situation; he shrugged and volunteered to get the ammunition. He backed to the end of the hedgerow and exited at a gate. He was now on a road that paralleled the hedgerow. At the next intersection he climbed through the break in the hedgerow and was followed by Lt. Ed Jansen. They both crouched on top of the hedgerow for a moment; it was like a situation without due caution that I had just experienced. Frank Ficarotta was shot in the head as he crouched on the high point of the hedgerow for too long a time. His lifeless body tumbled down the slope and he uttered not a word. He was dead. His face was purple. Tony Das, upon hearing of Frank Ficarotta's death said, "Oh Frankie boy." They were the best of friends. Infantry soldiers have little time to mourn. There were no more words to be said. Infantry soldiers can't, "heave their heart into their mouth."

Lt. Jansen was right behind him and the shot hit him in the stomach. Lt. Ed Jansen recovered to return to combat in the Operation Market-Garden in Holland, but he was wounded in the leg as the aircraft came under direct fire from the Germans. He jumped in spite of his wound which ultimately led to amputation and his death in 1994.

The complete story of Lt. Ed Jansen as related by Hilley Rosenthal is as follows: "On the flight over the Netherlands, a shell went up through the floor of the plane, up his leg and out through his thigh. The guys in the stick put a tourniquet on his leg and jumped. The crew chief became frightened and locked himself in the aft section of the tail of the airplane."

The patrol entered several houses in Addeville, as individuals or in pairs, to continue the search for Germans and carry out our

Trial by Combat

mission, despite the fact that our fear was almost unendurable. We exited quickly and moved through the village under the cover of ditches alongside the road, high walls and hedgerows.

My investigation in a house led me past a window through which a German snipers high powered rifle shot glanced off the floor several feet to my right and struck the inside of my left knee, as I was in full stride. It felt like a sledge hammer blow as it entered, somewhat spent. I pulled the bullet from the five layers of clothing, shook-off the concern for both the sniper and the blow, a superficial wound, until I could inspect it later. Brave men are wounded as readily as cowards because shell fragments don't care about the moral status of the soldier they penetrate.

* * * *

What was endurable, we endured because the nervousness of combat was like a malignant disease. You know it is there but you can't stop it from eating up your entire insides. You realize that all body functions are put on hold. Your lose weight, you lose sleep, but you love the pulsating sound of your rifle as it is fired.

Chapter 12

Assembly For La Barquette Lock

*"What counts is not necessarily the size of the
dog in a fight, its the size of the fight in the dog"*
                                        General Dwight D. Eisenhower.

The excitement lay just ahead and down the road. I could see the decomposed granite road, as it reflected a light brown color in spite of the puddles, in the early morning light. My energy pulled me in the direction of the field of action. It was the gathering of the 501st and 506th parachute infantry strays in an open field. They had been misdropped several hours before dawn.

Major Allen, in all of his feisty energy, was assembling all of these forces at Addeville, just two kilometers north and west of La Barquette Lock. The organizing of the parachutists was going well and small groups of parachutists who had commandeered farm equipment and been aided by French civilians, were sent into the surrounding fields (drop zones) to gather the parachuted equipment bundles that belonged to the squads. A good supply of arms and ammunition was sorely needed. We only had what we carried with us on the jump. An M-3 knife or a personal dagger will not do the job. During the bundle search we fought many small arms srikmishes with the Germans with few casualties. The farm cart yield was a bountiful supply of assorted military equipment-bric-a-brac. Some of it wasn't needed, so we discarded it, especially the gas masks. Hand grenades were the hot items.

At 1:30 A.M., earlier that morning, Colonel Johnson's plane load of warriors was delayed on their jump, when the green light flashed-"go." An equipment bundle was jammed against the bulkhead near the doorway, of the C-47 plane. The premature green light and the delayed jump was a cause of much concern and anxiety, for drop zone B was under water, which was just below. The delay and the speed in seconds put his plane on the forward edge of drop zone D. It was a major benefit. But to the colonel's disadvantage, his plane was illuminated by the Fortin farm fire, torched by the Germans; and that alerted the Germans to where he was landing. The exit from the aircraft after the bundle was catapulted out was routine. Colonel Johnson and his "stick" landed safely near their designated spot. This was fortunate because earlier, three teams of pathfinders who landed on drop zone D about 12:00 A.M. had been killed or captured. The Eureka-Rebecca signals had been foiled and the drop zone was not identified.

Colonel Johnson landed very close to Chateau Le Bel Enault. He roamed the darkness fighting several German riflemen at close range. As he made his way through ditches, canals and streams toward La Barquette Locks, he encountered small groups of 501st and 506th parachute infantry soldiers, the gathering of the eagles, all moving in the direction of the regimental objectives, bridges, roadways and the locks leading to Carentan.

In a very short time the group numbered about 150 and were well organized. As they came to the road junction, later known as "Hell's Corner," Colonel Johnson split the group into a large contingent of 100 and placed them in a defensive position at Peneme, facing the Utah Beach sector.

The remaining group of 50 made a dash from Hell's Corner, over a distance of 200 meters, across the lock to the south bank of the Douve River to fan out and dig-in defensive positions. During the rush, Private Campos was wounded by a German mortar shell but continued to advance.

This action set the next phase of 501st regimental objectives, which was to secure highway N-13, blow the four bridges leading to

Trial by Combat

Carentan at the top of the peninsula, and finally, destroy the railroad tracks leading to the port of Cherbourgh. This would prevent a German intrusion of armor and infantry into the 4 th Infantry Division landings at Utah Beach, only six kilometers to the north. The German fire from Carentan and from the surrounding area of the four bridges was light and sporadic but deadly.

The Americans were fortunate, in one respect, for if the Germans had opened the lock just before the Utah Beach landings, the resulting rush of water would have forced the 29th and 4th Infantry Divisions to land further north. This would have prevented them from using causeways 1, 2, 3, 4, which led to Ste. Mere Eglise. All beach supplies had to go through this city. The causeways which were held by the airborne regiments would thus be inaccessible to the beach forces. The timing was critical but the drainage was slow. As the result of the locks being closed the terrain was available to both the German and American forces. Both of them used this area alternately for offensive and defensive positions. As the invasion struggled through the initial phase, Germans and Americans fought to secure the four beach causeways.

Once the American troops were beyond the causeways, We realized that the Germans had placed a low priority on defending the La Barquette lock because they had mined the pastures. They also had German automatic gun positions, mortars and artillery defending all approaches to Carentan only three quarters of a mile away and three hundred feet above sea level. They gave accurate and destructive quality fire power from their gun batteries. They had registered their artillery on all possible targets during the military occupation of the previous four years.

Circa noon, June 6, 1944. Word soon got to Colonel Johnson at Hell's Corner, La Barquette Lock, Peneme area that Major Allen at Addeville, to the north, was assembling a sizable well- armed force of mixed paratrooper units who were itching to get into a fire fight. Colonel not only felt, but he knew that he needed reinforcements to complete the 501st Regimental D - Day objectives by attacking bridges, highways, railroad right of ways and to secure the southern boundary of the Cotentan Peninsula.

Earlier in the morning of June 6th, Colonel Johnson sent demolition patrols to the bridges that cross highway N-13 with instructions that the bridges were to be blown in order to prevent tanks for reinforcing the German positions that led to Carentan. The patrols returned with information that the area was too heavily defended. A more sizable force was needed to destroy the bridges. Colonel Johnson immediately took a force of fifty men and proceeded north to Addeville to make contact with Major Allen, who with a hundred men were already engaging the Germans of the 6th Parachute Battalion, as was Lt Col. Ballard at Les Droudries, about one half mile west of Addeville.

Colonel Johnson, by SCR radio, ordered Lt.Colonel Ballard to break off contact and the fierce engagement with the Germans and proceed to Addeville as soon as possible. The plan was that Johnson's, Ballard's, and Allen's forces would converge and form up to march from Addeville to Peneme to capture and destroy the bridges and to stop any German armored counterattack from the south against Utah Beach.

However, Colonel Ballard notified Colonel Johnson that it was impossible for him to disengage. There was a strong German contingent of the 6th Parachute Battalion behind him and Major Allen at Addeville. Nevertheless Johnson realized that he still had to proceed to the distruction of the bridges and seal the peninsula. Colonel Johnson, now at Addeville, drew Major Allen's forces and his own, in intending to attack the bridges.

Colonel Johnson's order came swift and clear, "Drop your mussette bags and extra equipment. Stay light."

All of our equipment was piled in neat rows in the pasture. We were never to see our possessions again. We prepared for the movement under the command of Colonel Johnson as quickly as possible. Addeville was located on a small hill which was under observation from the artillery at Carentan.

As we moved speedily, there were many thoughts racing through my mind. All hell was breaking loose around me on that blood-soaked peninsula, and thousands of men were being slaughtered and torn apart by the dogs of war; but all I can remember thinking about was the loss of my one pound block of maple sugar. The sugar

Trial by Combat

had been given to me by my girl friend's mother, just before I went overseas. It had only been tasted and showed two teeth marks. It must last forever but now it was gone forever.

As we moved off of the hill (Addeville) and out in the open, we were under the observation of the German artillery gunners in Carentan. Fortunately for us, at that time, the Germans could not determine whether we were friend or foe.

By the time we arrived at Hell's Corner, just 200 meters from La Barquette lock, the Germans were still unable to identify us. They were not sure of the identification because the German 6th Parachute Regiment was under orders by their commander Colonel Heydte, to move up highway N-13 from Periere and get to Carentan as soon as possible. The Germans were now moving in behind the few men that Major Allen had left to aid the reduced rear guard, at Addeville.

The German 6th turned left (east) to go beyond the inundated areas to reach Carentan. The Carentan Germans did not know that Colonel Johnson had left a small defensive force at Peneme.

They also did not know that Colonel Johnson and Major Allen had moved their entire force from Addeville south to reinforce their lightly held positions fronting the numerically superior force of German paratroopers at Peneme /La Barquette area.

This augmented force observed that a German battalion was moving south to the American front. The Germans were moving on foot in a southerly direction with Utah Beach on their left and a swampy area on their right. Ahead of them was Carentan. The German artillery unit in Carentan observed the movement of troops, but identification was still blurred. They had not sorted out the combatants.

From the American position, it appeared that the Germans in Carentan didn't see the approach of their comrades, but we saw them leisurely walking without flank-guards and their rifles slung on their shoulders. We heard them singing their national anthem.

Colonel Johnson and Major Allen immediately reconstructed their defense at Peneme, with more fire power. The rear guard left behind at Addeville by Major Allen had moved up to join the defensive force which now numbered somewhere between 150 to 190.

As the remnant of Major Allen's force lined the road at Hell's Corner, the German 6th Parachute Battalion turned right or west of the grassy, marshy polders laced with canals, to reach Carentan to rejoin their regiment in defense of their strategic city. As the German forces closed upon us, it was clearly seen that we were outnumbered, and neither force had enough fire power for a sustained battle. All of their weapons were rifles and light machine guns, but we had the mortars, machine guns, and hand grenades. Colonel Johnson ordered that fire be held until the Germans moved closer to our defense line. The hapless Germans were being scrutinized by Colonel Johnson's enraged engaged, entrenched reinforced airborne strays as they leisurely crossed the canals, not suspecting that they were moving into an ambush. The advancing Germans were surrounded by our bent flanks and trapped. Nervous and overeager G.I.'s, not under control of their own or any officer, started rapid fire with rifles, machine guns and mortars. The slow moving German formation was raked with devastating fire before they could hit the ground. The Americans began yelling for The Germans to surrender. The German Colonel said, "It's too early in the day." Colonel Johnson then went out, in the killing zone, with a cease fire order carrying a white bed sheet flag, with two German speaking G.I.'s, Nicholette and Blanchette, with surrender instructions to the German paratroopers. All German wounded were to place their bayonets on their rifles, plant them in the ground and put their helmets on the butt of their inverted rifles. This would aid in the identification of the German wounded.

As Colonel Johnson and his two aides returned to the Peneme defense line, they were fired upon again. The enraged G.I.'s returned the fire killing even more Germans. A half hour later, a second attempt was made by Colonel Johnson and Leo Runge, which resulted in a gradual trickle, then a large movement of surrendering German paratroopers.

The German artillery observers at Carentan were still unable to distinguish between the Americans and Germans fighting some 3/4 of a mile away. The German prisoners were milling about as their

Trial by Combat

surrender rate increased. They were disarmed and they huddled in a group out in the open, under the command of Captain Mc Reynolds of the Major Allen group.

The German gunners, desperately trying to help their troops, now let loose a barrage of artillery and mortar fire, all falling directly upon the captive Germans. Captain Mc Reynolds was killed as were many Germans.

With their battle line falling apart and so many of their comrades dead, wounded, and surrendering, the fire fight soon dwindled down into sporadic aimless potshots from the remaining fanatic hold outs.

When the fire fight at Peneme was just beginning, Father Sampson, at Addeville, 1/2 mile north of Peneme, early in the afternoon of D-Day, started receiving American wounded from other fighting in the area.

He learned of Colonel Johnson's movement of troops from Addeville to Peneme. He would now have to care for the non-ambulatory wounded left behind. At the same time another German Parachute detachment was overrunning the undefended Addeville. Father Sampson stood in the door with a white flag and identified himself as a clergyman. The Germans searched and searched the wounded for weapons. They found none. Father Sampson was put under guard and marched down the road a quarter of a mile, put against a wall and readied for execution, by several German paratroopers. With their rifles raised, moments later, a German officer ordered the executioners to halt. The officer snapped to attention and displayed his religious medals to the dismay of the executioners. Father Sampson's life was spared. He returned to the wounded in the near-by demolished aid station. For morale purposes, he isolated the dying in another room. He cooked, changed bandages, administered plasma and prayed.

* * * *

ACTION AT LA BARQUETTE LOCKS - REVIEWED This whole area around Addeville, Peneme, and La Barquette Lock was in a state of utter confusion almost amounting to chaos. The tail end of Colonel Johnson and Major Allen's forces including me, not yet placed on the defense line, were in the shallow roadside ditches in the open. They had observed all of the previous action. As slaughter was mounting, shells were hitting only yards from me. The only protection for my ears, from the sound of concussion, was my helmet. As the barrage increased, mud and canal water was splattered all over the road and I thought the next shell would be my last one.

Next to me, on the road, was Lt. Farrell, a naval fire control officer and Lt. Parker, an artillery forward observer from the 101st Airborne Division. Both had jumped with the 501st regiment. They had been ordered by Colonel Johnson to put fire on the German 6th parachute detachment entering Addeville behind us. Lt. Farrell made radio contact with the U.S.S. Quincy, standing off in the English Channel, via a complicated system of self-identification and relaying of coded radio message. The eight inch naval gunnery shells whistled over my head sounding like a speeding freight train. Father Sampson's aid station was again in jeopardy. I could see plumes of smoke from shells that were long and short of the target as Lt. Parker made intricate adjustments. Then came "fire for effect," with a high explosive shell from the cruiser. We all wondered if Father Sampson in the aid station could survive that terrible American barrage. Addeville erupted with sounds of fury and the smell of cordite from the exploding shells. The rear German attack was slowed down.

The German mortars and artillery in Carentan, which had been bombarding the cross road at 'Hell's Corner' were put under fire from the U.S.S. Quincy by Lt. Farrell at the request of Colonel Johnson. This brought some relief from the killing bombardment. The citizens of Carentan never forgave us for the destruction of their city and the death of family members. It is still June 6, 1944, late afternoon.

After the initial Hell's Corner fire fight, after the artillery shelling from Carentan, after the U.S.S. Quincy bombardment of Addeville, Tony Das, George Zeberowski and I were sent to cross the lock and search out the Parey farm house (lock keepers home) and barns for any lurking German snipers or strong points. Apparently no other

Trial by Combat

American forces knew that we had been ordered to do this. A 506th Parachute Engineers Demolition squad was at Brevands, about a quarter of a mile away, toward the English Channel coastline. The demolition squad was supposed to investigate the lock area by a night patrol, but they didn't do it. This could have caused us some trouble if the Germans had moved in behind us, but fortunately they didnot Our mission was to set up a strong point, observing all approaches to the lock. The remnants of the 6th German Parachute Battalion would be coming our way if they veered from their intended path, to reach and reinforce Carentan, and if they escaped our defense line at Peneme. They would be descending upon us like wolves on the fold.

At the Claude Parey farm, the strong points weren't in any of the buildings. I decided that we should set up in a corner of the vegetable garden extending to the right side of the farm house. This would give us the broadest view of the terrain, looking toward Carentan across the mine field and a marshy polder. The Madeleine and Jordan Rivers curved like an oxbow to our front, the Douve River was behind us and in front of the farm house. These were natural obstacles against German patrols.

If they came, they would be funneled into the area we were ordered to protect. The Jordan and Madeleine Rivers were both about twenty feet wide and about ten feet deep, and flowed into the Douve River downstream.

On the bank of the Jordan River, closest to us, we pounded in the ground about ten feet apart several three foot stakes. Three strands of baling wire were connected to the stakes. Tin cans were suspended from the wire, at varying heights. Each can contained several pebbles or iron bolts and nuts. The trip wire device was angled about forty-five degrees from our foxholes toward the river. The beginning and the ending couldn't be seen in the dark. There was only one way through it, for we had command of the battlefield. If a German patrol contacted the alarm trip wire device in darkness, we knew that an engagement would take place. We expected a number of enemy night patrols would be made into the dark area of the lock perimeter, June 6-7. If a German patrol walked up to the Parey farm from the south and west of Brevends, they would set off the alarm. Tony Das, George Zeborowski and I had dug foxholes just inside of the vegetable garden. The three foxholes formed a right angle in the corner. Each of us was connected by a parachute suspension line tied to our wrist. One stayed awake for two hours, while the others dozed. We rotated the sentry duty during the hours of darkness. A jerk of the line would alert the other two, for we knew what to expect. We also decided to maintain absolute silence during hours of darkness because we were so close to the river bank. As we waited, the only sounds we could hear were the peeping of night insects and the booming of distant guns.

At 2:00 A.M., a German patrol walked up to the Parey farm house, bypassed the barn and set off the alarm. With a jerk of the suspension line, all three of us cut loose with a fusillade of fire from one Thompson machine gun and two M-1 rifles. A number were wounded but escaped. One of the wounded lay near the trip wire fence, about fifty feet from our foxholes. At times he was yelling and at times he was moaning well into the remaining hours before dawn. He evidently couldn't walk or crawl away because the sounds came from the same spot. It was a low gurgling sound of a dying man, one that stops all conversation. We hoped he would die and give us some relief. We also thought it might be a ruse to entice us to investigate and shoot or capture us. The gurgling continued for several hours more. Finally (Name withheld) could stand it no longer. He slowly crawled out to the dying man and finished him off with his M-3 jump knife. We let the German lie there until dawn and walked out and dragged him into the garden. We put him in a shallow prepared grave, face up. We could then envision everything about his last painful night. He was about thirty years old. He didn't fit in the grave. It was too short. (Name withheld) jumped on his ankles, which were stuck on the edge of the grave, several times to pound them into the soft wet earth.. We took the German paratrooper's pay book and identification tags from around his neck, leaving one on his body wedged between his teeth. The other one we tied to a cross fashioned out of branches, which we placed at the head of the grave. He was covered and we mounded the dirt, and an additional piece of colored cloth was tied to the cross to attract attention. The pay book and remaining insignia were turned

Trial by Combat

into battalion at the earliest opportunity. I didn't want to go into combat again with German identification in my possession. The insignia identified the German soldier as a member of the German 6th Faslleschrimjagers (91st Air landing Battalion).

The burial of the German soldier happened early in the morning of June 7. It was actually my final action against the enemy on D-Day. Many have called it The Longest Day. It certainly was a long terrible day, but there were too many more long and miserable days to come before we left Normandy.

Chapter 13

Capture Of Carentan

I have regarded the forward edge of the battle field as the most exclusive club in the world.
                            General Byron Horrocks (British)

Carentan was a thriving city of 10, 000 (1944). Its approach was by highway N-13 and a railroad that terminated at the port of Cherbourgh. Carentan lay at the bend of the Douve River and was surrounded by marsh land to the north toward Ste Come du Monte, Addeville and Veriville triangle. The water exit of the Douve River to the English Channel was through the Grand Vey, just south of Le Madeleine and Poupville. (see map). General Maxwell Taylor, commanding officer of the 101st Airborne Division, was ordered by the IV Corps to expedite the capture of Carentan, which was already behind schedule. Carentan was the north-south link solidifying Utah and Omaha Beaches. The link -up must be made immediately to make the lodgement, the unification of Omaha and Utah beaches secure. General Taylor decided to attack Carentan from three directions simultaneously. The 327th Glider Infantry (which went in by glider on June 6th) would attack from the north. The remaining 327 th Glider Infantry, which came in by landing craft from Utah

Beach, would attack from the west through the Escart Canal region. The 501st Parachute Infantry would attack from the northeast. The 506th Parachute Infantry would undertake a forced night march, swinging around Carentan to the southwest. The 502nd Parachute Infantry would fight its way down highway N - 13 from the four bridges at Ste Come du Monte. The coordinated attack would begin at dawn, June 12th.[1] Carentan had to be Kraut disinfected- cleansed and sanitized. The 501st opened the attack by crossing the area from Peneme-Douve River Estaury. This was a low-lying river marsh covered by mine fields. During the early evening, we started our trek and attack through the mine fields. It was harrowing but without incident. We were again under constant observation by the artillery gunners in the Carentan cathedral, but no fire came our way because it was thought that the Germans were evacuating their positions to form a new defense line from which they could counterattack. Our path was a zig-zag trail and only eighteen inches wide. Our greatest fear would be a misstep outside of the small skull and cross bones burgee yellow flags mounted on red steel rods that marked the way. These flags were placed by German engineers for the safe return of German patrols and we hoped that no wiley German had changed the placement of the markers in anticipation of our coming. We walked in each other's footsteps as long as we could see them, so as not to set-off a shu mine (S - mine). Once we were out of the mine field, we were routed around Carentan to the north, toward Le Billionaire. With the pressure of the 327th Glider Infantry and the 502 nd and 506th Parachute Infantries, progress was rapid.

   A heavily fortified German command post was located in a farm house surrounded by hedgerows and a cabbage patch. Colonel Cole, commander of the 502nd Parachute Infantry Regiment, was ordered to take that position. After calling in smoke shells, Colonel Cole ordered his men to fix bayonets and charge the entrenched enemy. The fierce bloody fight that ensued is often referred to as the Battle of the Cabbage Patch.

---

1 The coordinated attack will begin at dawn. Bando, The 101st Airborne division At normandy pge.119.

Trial by Combat

Despite heavy casualties on both sides, the position was taken and highway N-13, the strategic route between Cherbourgh and Carentan, was open.

After the 502nd fight in the cabbage patch, the weakened German artillery forces and the remnants of the 6th German Parachute Infantry Battalion were driven out of Carentan and attempted to reassemble with other German units to prepare a counterattack. Carentan was finally occupied and liberated but not without significant civilian loss of life.

Company C dug into a defensive posture on the back side of Carentan facing east. We dug our foxholes with care and trepidation. Expecting a series of counterattacks, Company C prepared a series of patrols of 4 to 6 men for the sole purpose of probing enemy outposts.

The two men who lead a patrol are called scouts. There is nothing between them and the whole damned German army but the muzzles of their rifles.

The password out and beyond our listening posts and strong points was "water-belt." We had no maps of the area out and beyond 1 1/2 miles. Combat wisdom was our only security. Each nightly patrol was lightly armed and the patrol leader carried a 536 walkie talkie radio, which when turned on crackled and popped. Silence, stealth, and movement by hand signals characterized our probe. We were to avoid taking any prisoners or getting into a fire fight. Just observe their movements on their outpost line of resistance and location of weapons. Not a tough job. It made for good activity, if you were combat-wise.

The first patrol started out about 11:00 P.M., June 17. They returned in a very short time with a casualty-Gene Acevedo. A hand grenade exploded in Gene Ascevedo's left pants pocket and the fragments were deeply imbeded in his thigh. The patrol was aborted and they safely crossed the out post line.

Another patrol was mounted about 2:00 A.M. the next morning to locate any enemy strong points. I was ordered to lead the patrol of three men lightly armed and to carry a walki-talkie radio and move rapidly. Our weapons were M-1 rifles and a Thompson machine gun and plenty of ammunition. The pass-word remained the same.

As we passed out of our area, we identified ourselves by name so our strong points could recognize our voices. They were to pass the word along to the relieving strong point if we were not back within the allotted time. We explained our mission. How long we would be gone and how far out we would patrol. Our final request was, "Keep your airways open." The departing formation was one scout in the lead, about 10 to15 yards ahead of me followed by two others staggered on opposite sides of the road. The quarter inch copper power lines and concrete power poles were down and entwined the roadway for hundreds of yards and crisscrossed our path. We had to step over them and in doing so we would contact a copper wire which sent a "twang" echoing into the darkness, ahead of us. We feared that this might alert the enemy. The route was bounded on both sides by dense woods, cordoned off by ditches and barbed wire fencing, which shredded the light of the moon. My patrol continued, without incident, about one mile beyond our listening post. Suddenly, the scout, Marvin Van Buskirk, signaled a halt for an observation and an investigation. A farm house was parallel and offset from the road about twenty yards on the left. An outhouse was in front and at the far end of the farm house. I came forward to the scout as the patrol crouched to wait for the next signal. The outline of a German soldier could be plainly seen as he stood rigidly several feet away from the house at its far end, but opposite the outhouse. We stood motionless without being seen. I noticed the soldier move toward the outhouse, so I challenged him. I yelled' "WATER" and the reply came back in German, even though I anticipated a French reply. Just then the creaking door of the outhouse was flung open and out stepped another German soldier. Van Buskirk and I cut loose with our weapons. No more was heard from the two German soldiers. Recognizing no other enemy movements, we slowly withdrew and opened up the 536 radio to report to the listening post that we were returning to our lines without casualties. Shortly, we passed our outpost, gave the recognition passwords, and entered the cocoon of safety. The patrol ended with a measure of success. We located an enemy installation. This meant that enemy troops were migrating and retreating from Omaha Beach, to the inland areas.

The next afternoon, Sunday, June 18, I took another patrol out on the same route with two other riflemen to observe enemy buildup, since the previous night's farm house encounter. The weather was warm, bright, and clear. The sun threw shadows of the trees across the road, flashes of light reflected from the downed copper power lines, and the smell of German cigarettes was in the air. But not a sound could be detected at the farm house.

We wanted to investigate beyond this point. We were aware that a German guard might be observing us, and might let us pass, figuring that a German sniper would get us further on. We followed the gradually curving road to the right for a half mile. A two story farm house and barn came into view on our left. Both were set back from the road about two hundred yards. In front of the buildings were a series of animal holding corrals, muddy and without vegetation. Two sets of corrals were separated by a road that led to the farm house from the frontage road.

A large gate, where it abuts the farm house road, caught our attention. This created a format for discussion. The three of us stood momentarily opposite the gate, in the middle of the road. We started to decide on a best plan, either to investigate the farm house or by-pass it. Before the discussion was concluded, Robert J. Kahoun took two steps toward the gate to determine if it was locked. If it was, we would by-pass the farm house. At that very moment, he crumpled silently to the ground. We never heard the shot that hit him. Realizing that he had been killed by a sniper, Van Buskirk and I crouched in line with the gate posts, even though they were small in diameter. We expected to hear a shot or machine gun fire, but none came. Both of us pulled Bob Kahoun into the ditch on the other side of the road. We watched the farm house and barn for any enemy movements for about ten minutes. Nothing was observed. Kahoun died instantly from a single bullet which was dead center, through his helmet into his forehead. The shot was fired at a distance of about two hundred to two hundred fifty yards from the buildings, with smokeless powder. The sniper used a telescope sight and a silencer to kill Pvt Robert Kahoun. The German was well concealed and most certainly planned a route of escape and did so immediately.

It was too dangerous to carry Robert out of the area and retrace our incoming route, because we feared if there were any Germans at the farm house that we passed on the patrol the night before, they would be waiting to ambush us. We took the return route through the dense forest as a protection, and exited far below the farm house to avoid any entrapment. After crossing into our lines, I informed the outpost that a rifle squad, medic and a jeep was needed to return Bob Kahoun. The retrieval took place without an incident.

Inside and front center of Bob's helmet was a black ace of spades playing card. The bullet had entered the card dead center. Marvin Van Buskirk told us that "Just before we took off for the Normandy invasion from England, Bob cut a deck of playing cards, and decided that whichever card came up he would place it in his helmet for good luck- it was an ace of spades."

Fifty years later, the account of Robert J. Kahoun's death while on patrol was related to his brother, John Kahoun by me. This brought to conclusion the many confusing accounts of Robert Kahoun's death.

On Sunday morning, June 19, 1944, before another patrol was mounted to scout enemy territory, Catholic mass was said by Father Sampson, our regimental Catholic Chaplain. He used the hood of a jeep as an alter and covered it with the canopy of a camouflage parachute. About thirty of us were present to hear mass in a small field on the slope of the bald part of Hill #30, just outside Le Billionaire. Evidently the Germans were preparing a counterattack preceded by an artillery barrage. We could hear the shells coming in but they were long. Soon the range was shortened and we were under fire. Father Sampson told us to return to our companies, but we dug in deeper and he continued with the mass. Over a period of about thirty minutes, there were thirteen duds that struck the ground harmlessly within killing range. After the mass, we returned to our companies comforted and inspired. We knew that God had a hand in it. Further more, the counterattack never materialized. We had been blessed even though sadness had enveloped us with the loss of Robert J. Kahoun. Father Sampson was so heavenly-minded and so earthly-good that he became a legend in the 501st Regiment. He was a silent partner in the institution of death.

Trial by Combat

_Father Sampson's exploits have been told in books, movies, and television specials. He is universally praised and admired. We Airborne soldiers like to believe that he represented the best of our kind, because he was one of us, but we realize that his spirit and courage could be found in many of the tens of thousands of Allied troops who, against incredible odds, smashed through the almost impregnable defenses and drove the vaunted German forces out of Normandy.

In this chapter I have tried to relate my own personal experiences in that battle. I have not tried to present the macro view, the 'big picture' of that history-making event. For one thing, I was only one small speck in the big picture; but, more importantly, the battle was so complex, the confusion was so widespread, and the mishaps were so numerous, it was impossible to comprehend the entire situation.

In order to get some idea of the scope of the Normandy battle, it would be useful to read the accounts of many of the soldiers who fought there. In the next chapters I have included the experiences of three of my comrades.

Chapter 14

The Longest Week Captain Robert H. Phillips Vice President
Trust Company of Georgia

Note: some of the text is not readable.

I am inspired to account for my personal experiences and that of 17-18 paratroopers of the 101 st Airborne Division, during the invasion of Europe for several reasons;
1. To know whether or not I could write an interesting account of "cops and robbers" type of battle.
2. To hurry after 15 years to get the account down before I forget them.
3. To try to state the facts as best I remember them before the stories get better with age and telling.
4. Each "D-Day" serves as a reminder and then I question why I have not written these experiences.

Actually I have been besieged by too many people to relate them. The reading of the Longest Day serves as a pretty good shove. Our experiences were repeated by a good many small groups, no doubt. But I haven't read of them as recounted by those who have experienced them. So I decided to give it a try.

Perhaps some background will give the reader the "Big Picture" and the relationship to the "smaller picture."

The 101st Airborne Division was stationed in England at a number of different locations. Several days before the invasion date or early in June of 1944 the 501st Parachute Infantry Regiment moved to a marshaling area surrounded by fences at a British airdrome (Merry field Airport), and security with no contact with the outside world.

Each unit commander was shown the objective assigned to him in the highly secret war room. It was guarded every minute, both day and night. Commanders entered only when bidden to do so. (Bigoted) Several days were devoted by the unit commanders, of which I was one, to study their assignments and formulate detailed plans. Each individual member was thoroughly briefed on the detailed plans of his unit.

Only general information was given as to the missions of the Regiments of the 101st Airborne Division. The 101st Airborne Division was assigned to capture the locks at the Douve River (La Barquette Locks) and destroy the main highway bridges northwest of the city of Carentan. My company's mission was to seize and secure the road junction south of St Come du Monte, a small village thus securing the flank of the drop zone (Drop Zone -D). This position overlooked the main highway bridge north of Carentan and later gained the name of "Deadman's Corner."

The story begins in one C - 47 transport. The first plane of Company C, 501st Parachute Infantry Regiment of the 101st Airborne Division, sometime between 12;30 A.M.-1:30 A.M. D - Day, June 6, `1944. I was company commander of Company C, but as it turned out I wasn't to rejoin that until a week had passed.

As I remember it required 9 C-47 planes to transport a parachute infantry company (128 paratroopers) and its assigned ammunition and equipment. Each plane was assigned from 17-20 men plus the aircraft crew depending on how many men might be attached to the unit to carry out its special mission. The group was called a "stick." We were assigned to jump on drop zone D which appeared to be only 1 1/2 miles north of Carentan. Well over half of those planes failed to drop their loads on the assigned drop zone. The main reason, I believe was the unfamiliarity of the pilots with dropping parachutists at night. I am sure many had participated in practice jumps at night, but I doubt the live flak fire was simulated.

Trial by Combat

A number of planes were shot down, some dropping personnel in inundated areas where many drowned, which wascertainly no fault of the pilots. Many parachutists were killed because they were dropped specifically where they belonged, but ironically the enemy was there and waiting.

Although assembly of parachutists on the ground was hazardous and disorganized, this very condition served to confuse and stupefy the enemy and probably resulted in many more men living to fight on D-Day than if they had been dropped just according to plan.

I didn't know actually exactly where our particular plane dropped. But it was south of Carentan, and from recollections from discussions with Frenchmen and review of one of our maps during the trip back to our objective, I believe we were 10-12 miles from Carentan. I estimated we covered 20-25 miles in a very circuitous route to finally reach Carentan.

During the next several days units were gradually picking up scattered elements, and men had attached themselves to other units until they could rejoin their own. All were trying to carry out their assigned missions. I guess that very few carried out their assigned missions as conceived, but the assignments were carried out after various changes and improvisations. That was another reason for the success: the flexibility and ability to changes plans under almost any circumstance. We were highly mobile. We fought with what we carried and we carried enough for several days on our own.

Our "stick" was composed of 17 men. I was the stick leader and the last man in the stick was Sergeant Barney, supply Sergeant of company C.L.F. Hansen, Headquarters company 1st Battalion was the last man out the door. I came across Sergeant Beall's body grave several hours after the jump. I lost my helmet on the jump. Four 1st Battalion company commanders were either wounded or captured solo and were taken to St George Bohon church. Joining the group was Major Phillip Gage, Captain Paty, Captain Simmons, ___?___ ___?___ _____?_, _____?_ about 5 E M's (enlisted men), First Sergeant _____? on site (text is unknown).

We had received a red warning signal in the plane (preparation to go). Sergeant Bealls, Operation Sergeant and I had the responsibility of dumping out the ammunition and equipment bundles just before jumping and before the green light signaled jump. Those lights were immediately over the door. As we pushed the bundles close to the door, the cover of the parachute pack at one end broke open. The parachute bellowed in and out of the plane. We desperately kicked the bundle out of the door, grabbed the next bundle, and as it was in position I saw the green light go on, the signal to jump. I yelled the command "GO," and with that we shoved the last bundle and dived out behind it. Apparently we were off to a confused start and sixteen men followed. I didn't see them because it was very black. This was like a number of other night parachute jumps we had made except for the flak. Confusion and fear resulting from the knowledge that we were to engage an enemy on the ground, gripped us.

I saw Sergeant Barney about three days later and saw Sergeant Bealls grave about two weeks later. He was buried by the Germans according to our prisoners. I didn't see any of the others until after the war. As I hit the ground I ripped the combat knife from my leg scabbard and frantically cut my harness off my body. I fully expected somebody to run up or by but there was none. I got my carbine and other equipment ready and started a lonely reconnaissance. Sometime later, as I crossed a field, I felt an impact on my left hip as though I had been swatted by a big flat board. This was it! I hit the ground knife out, grenade in hand, and crawled back in the direction from where the disturbance originated. I never found the source.

After much reconnaissance, consuming about an hour or so, I settled down in the center of a hedgerow with the carbine across my legs and waited. A short time later, I saw some figures floating toward me. I waited until I saw the luminous discs on the front of their helmets. I snapped my cricket and got a welcoming cricket reply. I then asked them who they were Lt Bowser, Sergeant Arneson, a Mexican lad from our company, and one other made up our group. It must have been about 4:00 A.M. In the morning. We were all scared but glad to have some more strength. We attempted to reconnoiter a house nearby by batting on the door. But the Frenchmen who answered was so scared he refused to help. So with dogs barking and door bells ringing and with daylight approaching, we struck out across the fields staying off the road.

Trial by Combat

I was just in the process of taking off my mussette bag and getting a drink from my canteen cup, too late, it was blown wide open and there was a scorched area of about one foot in diameter in my jacket. This was the result of some missile fired at me earlier that morning. Just at that moment I raised my head above the hedgerow and I saw a group of 18-20 German soldiers on the double rushing past. I faded down and motioned the rest to be quiet.

That was our first look at the enemy. I decided then and there that our primary mission was to get back to my unit, 501st Parachute Infantry Regiment, alive with these men. I didn't know what skills that would require or what problems we would encounter, but one thing was clear. We were in the midst of the enemy and could count on no help but that of God and our resources. Perhaps the circumstances were such that we never had to encounter such a proposition, but we did engage the enemy on numerous occasions, at close quarters. We were steathly, cautious, and bold at the proper times. The days that followed were filled with excitement, fear, and heroism. The nights were really cold. There were no blankets. The only body protection was our cotton jump suits and any camouflage cover, hedgerows, bushes, gullies. Actually there was little sleep. Each night was one of dozing, cat-napping and constant checking of our posted sentinels. Our feet were always cold. In other words we lived life armed because we had to and were glad every moment to be alive.

We kept moving during the day at first, then finally at night because the Germans were thick and everywhere. We were so excited it was impossible to confer with French farmers sufficiently to get any valuable help. Later on, that changed as we became calmer and picked up a few company men who spoke French.

We sought out several village priests who spoke English. We found a fellow by the name of Murphy on D +1, an A company man, I think, out in a field. He was moaning and he thought his ankles were broken. He wanted to wait for the Germans to capture him. I insisted that he go with us. We taped his ankles and dragged him with us. On the last day Murphy was walking pretty well. We soon picked up two more men. We just came upon them in a field. They looked baffled and wild-eyed. We gathered ammunition boxes from parachutes hanging in trees.

At about D +3, we ran into Sergeant Barney, who had 7 C company men with him. They told of having seen Lt. Hutchenson shortly thereafter, and he had 4 or 5 men with him. We had several skirmishes with small groups of Germans, not drawing any blood that I know of.

After the first several days of shock, we began to get our bearings. At night a patrol of 4-5 men would move out to the road where traffic was noticeable The patrol would ambush vehicles by means of Hawkins mines. Horses and ammunition carts would go sky high after running over the mines. After the patrol returned, I assigned another patrol, always cautioning them to stick close to one another and not to get far-out from the hide-out, which was always in the woods.

Our strength grew from 4 in the early darkness to 17-18. Finally there were two officers besides myself, several sergeants and the rest were privates. There were 5 or 6 of us from Company C, 3 or 4 from Company B, several from Battalion Headquarters, and several from other units. For control purposes, I decided it would be best to divide the group in half, placing Lt.Hutchenson in charge of one group and Lt. Bowser the other group. Sergeant Barney worked closely with both and immediately established himself as a leader of men. Lt. Hutchenson was one of the most courageous and gutsy men I had ever seen. He liked to roam by himself at night and I cautioned him several times against repeating his dangerous missions. Eventually he was the only man we were to lose.

Just before joining Lt. Hutchenson and Sergeant Barney, our small group encountered a small enemy patrol among a group of houses surrounding a courtyard including a barn. I passed through an archway between several buildings and came face to face with a German. We were both completely surprised. I ducked back and pulled out a hand grenade and peeked around the corner of the building. The kraut was no more than 15 feet away. He was preparing his potato masher (grenade). I heaved my grenade and started running back toward the houses. Moments later several of us were trying to pick-off Germans who were crawling and whose

Trial by Combat

heads, were bobbing up and down in the wheat field. I could never quite zero on any one of those heads and they were clad only with cloth overseas caps. We disengaged as silently and mysteriously as we had come together.

Our most harrowing experiences started with our arriving in a small enemy village. I guess it was about D + 3 or 4. We found a farm house on fairly commanding ground. We were fed some very full salad, wine and bread by the family, but that was the extent of it. Half of the group stayed on the ready and rested. The other half moved down to the village main crossroad about 400-500 yards away and proceed to set up a shooting gallery. They shot up several armored cars and trucks. An occupant of one of the vehicles was an officer. The vehicles were caught at close range by our machine gun fire.

We were so loaded with ammunition and guns that walking was a real chore. After we pulled all personnel back to the farm house, the village priest, who spoke English, appeared and warned us that the Germans were coming in force. We then stashed more than half of our ammunition and one of our machine guns in the loose hay in the barn and started across the fields. As we reached the largest open area adjacent to the farmhouse, I looked back and swarms of Germans were scouring the fields. We moved stealthily but rapidly to put distance between us. Somewhere and in some fashion, I can't possibly recall, I learned the Germans found our ammunition and burned the barn and the farmhouse to the ground.

As we approached a road, two German motorcycle messengers spotted us. We were surprised. They mounted the hedgerows and fired their schmeisers (automatic machine pistols) at random. No one was hit, but those two made our group hit the ground, so we immediately deployed one group swinging to the right and the other to the left in order to envelope them. They dropped down behind the hedgerow paralleling the highway and fired periodically. As I moved into another field and advanced with the left group, I came upon of sort of corral or fenced area with a gate that opened upon the road. As I was about 20-30 yards from the road, I saw a prone body paralleling the the road, about half of it exposed to the opening. I sighted my carbine from a post of the fence and pumped 2 or 3 rounds into the figure and then ran up to inspect. At the same time one of our group and a member of our company ran up. I turned this German over, and he appeared to be mortally wounded. He was a young blond and blood was running from his mouth and he cried "komarad" several times. The man on my left, in his excitement, shouted he was going to blow his head off. I told him he was mortally wounded and we wouldn't do that.

As we gathered on the road, we saw a truck-load of German soldiers riding down the road. I don't remember how many but they were ambushed. We caught them from a cross-fire from both sides of the road and they emptied fast. The Germans who weren't killed in the trucks were running down the road madly. One of our men jumped on the lead truck, using the machine gun mounted over the cab, opened fire on the krauts. The excitement was enervating and exhausting. I think it was now late in the afternoon, and I guess it was about D +4. We had run out of rations before the salad meal. We grouped together across the road, passed a farm adjacent to the road and passed into a field, probably 100 yards x 200 yards. It seemed to be a thicket dense with growth and loaded with thorns, possibly wild roses. Anyway we were literally fatigued. I felt we could bog-down and have a few winks.

Obviously the German patrols were on the move as we posted several sentries and spotted them. I had a feeling that this was going to be the place for a hand-to-hand encounter. An hour or so before dark some Germans had moved into position around the thicket. They raked the area pretty thoroughly with machine gun fire, fired some mortar rounds and made it seem like a big operation. The machine gun bullets were much to high to do any harm as we had the protection of the earthen base of the hedgerow, which surrounded all the small plots in Normandy. We just sat tight and silent. No fire was returned. The enemy ceased fire.

We manned two-man sentinel posts, about 3 or 4 at strategic points, alternating for the night. I remember Sergeant Barney was incharge of these posts. I got a lot of encouragement from his poise and determination. We remained there all night. The next morning there was evidence of the krauts. They either felt we had disappeared or they didn't care to make close contact. I guess this was now D

+ 5. We were bushed but I knew we were getting closer to north Carentan by the sound of the weapons. Each day we seemed to know only generally where we were. Discussions with French citizens were not satisfactory. They got too excited and couldn't tell us where were we were the map.

I am reminded of a funny but dangerous experience. We had several smoke bombs (orange) to signal our artillery as to our position so we wouldn't be mistaken for the enemy. On one afternoon we were getting close to Carentan, and one of the men suggested that we set off one of the smoke bombs we had. We did and barley lived to tell about it. Shortly thereafter an artillery barrage zoomed in on us. It was short but intense; needless to say we moved from the location with all haste. We learned we were somewhere near the town of Baupte, which is almost due west of Carentan. Quite suddenly and unexpectedly a small elderly Frenchman appeared through an opening in the hedgerow. He had a pail of milk, a long roll of bread under his arm, a small leg of pork. One of the men, a member of Company B, spoke some French and learned the old man knew we were in the area and knew we would be hungry. He apologized for the meager rations but he explained he was trying to help refugees who had fled from the north, where the fighting was heavier and more organized. I remember each man got a slice of bread and a half canteen cup of milk. We decided to hole-up for the day and move out at night.

The night came and we moved out in a single file. We actually moved very slowly with one arm on the shoulder of the man in front. We were cautious, silent and virulent. I was third or fourth man from the front. Sergeant Barney was at the rear. We moved and rested and spoke only in whispers. Late that night we came upon some German mortar positions. We actually felt the guns and heard the Germans crews snoring in their houses. There were no sentinels. We didn't bother to shoot the place up or toss hand grenades. Frankly it was so dark we would have scattered and shot-up a number of our own people.

We were reaching our ultimate goal and wanted to rejoin our units. Just before dawn, we pulled into a field and stretched out in a small gully paralleling the hedgerow, posted several sentinels and got a cat-nap. After several hours we decided to move on. We crossed a railroad, approached a farmhouse and a river. It turned out to be the Douve River. This was the river just north of Carentan and the bridge over it was a major battle area. We were about to move closer when the last man to cross the railroad tracks spotted a group of troops. We didn't know whether they were enemies or friends and could take no chance of guesswork. Here we were on the alert and faced with another thriller.

We crossed back over the railroad and at that point, it was in of a cut. There was a small type utility house at the railroad crossing. I gave preliminary orders as it was definite that this was a large group of Germans moving toward us. They were retreating, it appeared from Carentan. They appeared somewhat carefree, helmets off and sauntering along talking. My guess is that there were between 75 and 100 men. We deployed along the track on both sides of the house. Our aim was to destroy them all. This encounter started with opening fire on them from my hand signal, and was to result in Lt. Hutchenson's death. We opened up with one machine gun and each individual weapon firing simultaneously. If it weren't so deadly a business it would have seemed funny to see that mob scatter like a bunch of wild men. I assume our engagement lasted about 30 minutes. The Germans organized and started their attack. As they advanced on our position Lt. Hutchenson kept exposing himself. I was behind a small house. I cautioned him several times to observe from cover. The last time I saw him alive he had stepped out of the door of the house with a grenade in his hand, and, as he threw it, several Germans were as close as 20-25 yards. I saw him reel around. I was about 5 yards from him. He was hit in the stomach with what I thought was some sort of pistol grenade because he was ripped wide open. Just before this happened I had passed the word to the group to prepare to move out, since it appeared the Germans would envelope us. We had the river to our back and the only move we could make was a lateral one. I gave the command to retreat and the men began moving on the double to the other side of the tracks, parallel to them in the direction from which the Germans had come. I ran over to Lt. Hutchenson and took a quick look. He was done for. I ran back to the B Company man, who was the last man.

Trial by Combat

We both grabbed the machine gun-it was hot-and started running together to catch the others. The krauts were still firing but soon we left them behind.

We saw German and American machine guns and ammunition and other abandoned equipment all over the place. We soon approached a good sized town. It was Carentan, the objective of our regiment, which was to have been seized by D+1, but pretty much required the whole division, I think, to capture Carentan on or about D+5 or D +6. As we entered the town we smelled the stench of fire-burned homes and dead cattle which were lying bloated grotesquely in the fields with their feet in the air, as we entering the town. We saw craters the size of homes, apparently from naval guns off shore. I saw a group of children who had been caught by the artillery. This was the most shocking scene of the entire week. I tried to guide our column away from it.

We reported to division headquarters, and I reported as accurately as possible where we had been and what we had seen of the enemy. We weren't able to be of too much help as to the enemy positions and strength because we were constantly on the move. I learned from our regimental adjutant that we had suffered heavy casualties among men and officers.

I was the ranking officer to survive in the Battalion. That afternoon, I reported to take command of Company C because Lt. Jansen had been shot in the stomach by a sniper, along with private Ficarrota, who had been with him trying to drag some ammunition over a hedgerow, and was killed at the same time.

One and all of our feelings--it was great to be with our own, in strength. There was established rapport and respect of one another that no other experience could shape between men as did this one. I think it was D+6, and certainly it was The Longest Week in the lives of eighteen men, except for one, which it was the shortest.

Capt Robert H. Phillips
501 Parachute Infantry Regiment, Company
C, Company Commander

Chapter 15

D-Day Experiences Of Lieutenant Eugene D. Brierre

I was born January 4, 1924, in New Orleans, Louisiana; attended Gulf Coast Military Academy, 1933-1942. I received a commission as a Second Lieutenant June 12, 1942, at which time I was 18 years old. I was assigned duty at Camp Walters, Texas, June 12, 1942. While there, I volunteered for the paratroops and joined the 506th Parachute Infantry Regiment in Camp Toccoa, Georgia. Upon arriving in England, I was assigned to Company C, 501st Parachute Infantry regiment.

The 101st Airborne Division had just put out a bulletin requesting a Second Lieutenant to volunteer to serve with the Division Headquarters for the invasion of Normandy. Anybody interested was to contact Major Legere at Division Headquarters.

Major Legere told me I would be in charge of the M.P. platoon. My primary responsibility was to use the M.P. platoon to defend the Division Headquarters and to use all other members of Division Headquarters in defense of the geographical location of the Headquarters if necessary.

I was also to be available to go on any special patrols that General Taylor might request. I volunteered for the assignment and was accepted.

About three weeks before D-Day, Division Headquarters was moved to the airport located at Greenham Commons. This was near Newbury in the south of England. I was given "bigoted" identification. This authorized me to go to all map rooms to see and learn about all of the secret preparations for the invasion.

Our drop zone (D-Red) kept getting small shadows which we learned were tree posts which had been placed on all of our drop zones. Thereafter, we learned from the French Underground that wires were strung to the tops of the poles and our drop zones were mined and machine guns were placed at strategic spots.

We changed our drop zones three times, and on each occasion posts were placed on the new ones. We jumped on the third drop zone in spite of the fact that tree posts were there. Officers were instructed to give their men specific instructions on keeping their feet together, as they came into land, so as to hopefully avoid straddling the wires between the posts. We were also to instruct them as to the probability of mines on the drop zones and enemy machine gun positions.

Our plane was identified as plane #1. General Taylor had the honor of being the first one out of the door for the jump. We had radar under our plane which was to tie in with equipment on the ground on our drop zone.

With this oral history is a copy of the manifest of plane #1. Also in plane #1 was George Koskimaki, a radio man and a reporter from Reuters News Service. I wrote a letter to my father and mother on the plane and gave it to the reporter to mail it when he got the first opportunity. (Did this violate security?). General Eisenhower came to our field and visited the paratroopers at every plane.

I think there were two "dry runs" when we thought we were going for the money and did not.

Major Legere was the jump master and was going out the door right behind General Taylor. I was the assistant jump master and was to be the last man to leave the plane.

Normandy was the qualifying jump for General Taylor to entitle him to be a paratrooper, his fifth jump. He was a very large man and was not able to get into his parachute harness without help, which I gave him.

When our plane finally tookoff, it circled continuously until it got to several thousand feet. As the other planes were taking -off,

Trial by Combat

they continued in a circle, and it was like corkscrews going up in the air, which I could clearly see from the door. General Taylor had brought some pillows to lay on the floor of the plane and rest during the trip. He told me he was going to take the chute off and wanted me to be available to be sure to help him get it back on for the jump. He laid down on the floor and appeared to go into a deep sleep, for about half of an hour. We started to put his chute on thereafter and it seemed like it wasn't going to be possible. After a struggle of about 5 minutes we got him all hooked up.

When we got near the drop zone I inspected the parachute packs of every man in the plane to see that it wasn't fouled and the paratroopers were properly hooked up to the cable. They all were and I returned to the last man position in the plane.

As we neared the drop zone, I could see some tracer bullets through the side windows. I also could hear explosions. No bullets hit our plane. We got out of the plane and my chute opened. I saw tracer bullets going up in several places but none of them were coming toward me. They were coming from places close to where I had to land. I landed in a tree on the side of a hedgerow and my feet were about 6 inches from the ground. I had a knife on both ankles and a jump knife in the pocket of my jacket. I was not able to open the pocket because of my weight in the chute. I had my carbine on my right leg and a machine gun belt on my left leg. I wasn't able to lift either leg to get the knife out of either ankle. After about 5 minutes a tracer bullet came through my chute above my head. Some how I got the strength to bend my right leg and reach the knife on my right ankle and cut myself loose.

I headed in the direction I thought was the assembly point. After about ten minutes, I was challenged by General Taylor himself. He and I continued on to the assembly point. About twenty soldiers were all that gathered at the assembly point.

General Maxwell Taylor wasn't sure of our location and neither was General Tony McAuliffe. The three of us looked at a map inside of a hedgerow. All three of us had different ideas of our location. General Taylor sent out patrols north, south, east and west. My guess proved to be the correct location.

General Taylor decided that our small group would assist in taking causeway #1 (Poupville). We spread out with two columns going on either side of the road towards Poupville and flank guards on both sides of the road out in the fields. I was the lead man of the left flank guard. I think Major Legere was at the head of the column in the road. He was soon seriously wounded in the leg. A medic got to him about twenty minutes later. We did not have any trouble taking this little village. After taking the village, General Taylor ordered me to take a patrol to go out and make contact with the soldiers coming from the beach. Some Germans had been reported to be near the road heading toward the beach. I took eight men and we headed along a hedgerow about 50 yard east of the road. We got to a point where there was no more cover and started to head back toward the road, which seemed to be clear. At that time we were fired upon from the beach. I shot an orange flare up into the air to show that we were friends. The firing stopped and we could see the troops starting to come up the road. When we got to a bridge, about six Germans came out with their hands up and surrendered. I went to the road and met a Captain Mabry. I recorded on my watch the exact time that I met him. I think it was about 11:10 A.M. I brought Captain Mabry to General Taylor, who made a notation in his records of the time we arrived at his headquarters.

Division Headquarters then moved out to go to the new planned location, and upon arriving there, we found the building had already been set up as a hospital. General Taylor decided to move our headquarters into a home in the little town of Heisville.

I set up defenses around our headquarters. Things were fairly quiet at headquarters. After getting the defenses set up, I went into the attic of the farm house to get some rest. Shortly thereafter, just as I was about to fall asleep, I heard a terrific explosion which shook the farm house. Thereafter I learned that the Germans had dropped a bomb on the hospital, which they thought was our headquarters. Immediately thereafter, I set up my headquarters in a fox hole in the farm yard.

I made three patrols for General Taylor. We never did run into any live enemy. We did find many dead Germans. We cut off their insignia and brought these back to General Taylor. On my first patrol,

I noticed a wedding band on a dead German. I never gave it another thought. On the second patrol I passed over the same location and saw that finger of the dead German had been cut off. This shocked and angered me. I thought that out of respect for the dead soldier's family, that the ring should have been returned to his family.

After Poupville had been captured, I came into a house where a German was lying on the floor, his gun was near him. I almost shot him when I realized that he was seriously wounded. He signaled me to hand him something. I saw that he was pointing toward a rosary. I grabbed his gun and unloaded it and put it at the other side of the room. I then picked up the rosary and handed it to him. He had the look of deep appreciation in his eyes and began to pray, passing the beads through his fingers. I learned the following day that he died shortly after I discovered him.

I was given a battlefield promotion for my participation in the invasion.

Chapter 16

D-day Experiences of S/Sgt. Myron G. Sessions
June 6 - June 13, 1944

You asked me about my part in the Normandy and Holland Campaigns. I'll do the Normandy one first, June 6, 1944, as I remember it. I'll do it over a period of days as I remember new details.

We were in secured areas for 3-4 days, cyclone type fences and living in priamidal tents. I remember it rained a lot and hard. At times we stood in chow lines in the rain in raincoats, helmet liners, and overshoes. We used this same uniform for "short arm" inspection, but that wasn't a problem because we weren't allowed to leave the secured area. In other words, no contact whatsoever with the outside world. The one thing that stands out in my mind during the three days in the staging area was the record they played over the loud speaker. It was David Rose's Holiday For Strings. They played it over and over again. I liked the tune every time I heard it. It takes me back to the staging area.

As you know, I was a Staff sergeant of a rifle squad and I had eleven men to look after. We were all housed in one tent and we became a very close-knit group.

On the evening of June 5, 1944, we got the order to move out from the staging area to the airfield, where we were to depart to our objective - Normandy, between St. Mere Eglise and Carentan,

France. We began putting our equipment on and blackening our faces with charcoal. I carried the usual two chutes, gas mask, 2 days K rations, an M -1 rifle, a Thompson submachine gun, ammo for the guns, in all about two hundred pounds. My normal weight at that time was 185 pounds, so I weighed over 300 pounds at the time I entered the plane. I could hardly straighten - up because I was so weighted down with equipment.

Sergeant De Huff was the designated jump master and I was the assistant jump master. The jump master jumps first and the assistant jump master jumps last. There were 16 men in the plane and I was # 16 or the last man out. These were my squad (12) men.

Back to the staging area I can remember a briefing given by Lt. Col. Carroll over a sand table for officers and noncoms. Lt.Col Carroll had just designated the drop zone and said that the pathfinders would be dropped first and would roll a white bolt of cloth from the drop zone to the initial objective. Sgt. De Huff asked, "Suppose the pathfinders don't make it, or what if the bolt of cloth isn't there?" The Lt. Col's answer was terse, "The bolt of cloth will be there." We know that Lt. Col. Carroll was dead before he hit the ground and DeHuff's and my plane dropped us some 15 miles from where that bolt of cloth was supposed to be.

As I recall it was about 10:30 P.M. when we began loading the plane (my plane). Some planes were loaded earlier and some were loaded later. It took the planes 1 1/2 hours to rendezvous and get into formation to precede to the drop zone. It was still daylight when we loaded into the planes. The thing that stands out in my mind about the flight over was how uncomfortable I was and I really wanted to get out of the plane and shed some of my equipment. The first to go would be my two chutes, then my gas mask and I lost my M-1 rifle on the jump, so I got rid of much right away. I wasn't in the air very long after my chute opened. Since I was the last man out of the plane, I figured that I jumped at about 3-4 hundred feet. It seemed to me the chute opened and I hit the ground kinda hard at that. I got out of my chute and looked around. It was very dark. It was about 1:30 A.M. on June 6, 1944. There was a moon, but it was mostly obscured by clouds. I began to listen for other paratroopers so that could gather my squad together. Upon hearing a rustle in the

Trial by Combat

bushes, I used my clicker and got no response. I tried again but got no response. I fired a short burst from my Thompson sub-machine gun and all I got back was a moo-oo.

I began to move in the direction of the firing. When I would get close, if I heard the guttural sound of the German language I would move in the opposite direction. I did this until daylight, still not contacting anyone in my plane and, for that matter, no one at all except the enemy.

At about daylight I was moving across on open space in the forest. I attempted to jump a ditch but landed in the ditch. I landed on something in the ditch. I thought at first it was a log but much too soft for that. With that, the log began to move and it turned out to be Pvt. Paul Sanders of my squad. Now there were two of us to take on the German army. Sometime later early that morning, we ran into S/Sgt Clive Barney, the Company C Supply Sergeant.

Sometime later in that day we came upon a paved main road. We decided to stake it out and wait and see what would come along. Remember that we were in the middle of enemy territory and Germans were all around us. Before long a company of German bicycle troops came along. We opened up fire at almost point blank range. We didn't stick around to check the casualties. We did see them jump off their bikes and jump into the ditches along the side of the road. We had previously reconnoitered a route of withdrawal through some ditches and ravines. If the Germans could have chased and surrounded us we would have been captured, like so many of our buddies in Company C.

On the 3rd day, we ran into Captain Robert Phillips, our Company Commander, with 18 men. There was a lieutenant from B Company with this group, and how he got mixed up with C Company, I'll never know. He was the only casualty in our 7 day march back to join the company and the division. The lieutenant I spoke of was killed on the day we arrived at Carentan. The officer's name was Hutchenson. A group of enemy was being flushed out of Carentan with the main body of the division attacking from the north. Our band of 21 came in from the south. The lieutenant from B company got a rifle grenade in the stomach and that was all.

On the same day we started our trek north with Captain Phillips in charge. He led the column and put me last man, probably because I had a Thompson sub-machine gun with about 90 rounds of ammunition. We had one .30 caliber machine gun, which Phillips placed in the middle of the group. Our fire power was definitely limited. Most of the men had M-1 rifles and two officers had carbines and as you know the carbines were very limited in their effectiveness. My Thompson sub-machine gun was very effective at close range-.45 caliber. It made a small hole going in and a large hole coming out.

An aside to the story: Paul Sanders and Clive Barney were among the group of 21 and they often attended the reunions. On the 4th day or D+3, we came across a main road-two lanes paved and Capt. Phillips decided to set up a road block and wait and see what might come along. I remember Capt Phillips was very careful in placing his men in advantageous positions with a good field of fire. My job was to make sure no one came upon us from the rear. I was actually facing away from the road, that is until all hell broke loose. It wasn't very long until a big Mercedes truck came along with about a dozen Germans in the back of the truck. On a given signal, all 21 of us fired on the truck at the same time. The truck turned over and caught fire with most of the occupants killed or wounded. Two or three ran down the road and were gunned down before they got very far. We didn't stick around very long to count the casualties. We knew once we got back at the Germans, they would be looking for us.

D-4, we continued our trek north, moving mostly at night and holeing up in some secluded spot during the day and trying to catch some shut-eye. Food was another problem. When we jumped we carried two day's K rations. We were now on our fifth day out and getting pretty hungry. Capt. Phillips sent three us up to a French farm house to see if they could spare something to eat. We came away with a roasted leg-o-lamb. Divided among 21 robust paratroopers, it don't amount to much.

On D+4 night, the Germans came looking for us. We were well hidden in a forest away from the road. The Germans wouldn't go off the main road at night, and as a result we weren't discovered. The Germans would fire into the forest but fortunately they didn't

Trial by Combat

hit anyone. D+5, we were holed up in a small forest during the day. We shared whatever food we had left which was very little. Someone in the group had a squad cooker, about the size of a tennis ball can. We were allowed to fire this up and use the instant coffee packets found in our long - aged, used K rations. But some of us didn't save the packets of instant coffee. Normally we wouldn't drink the instant stuff if brewed coffee was available. But we hadn't had brewed coffee for a week, so the instant was delicious.

D+6, we continued to move in the direction of Carentan. As we approached the town of Carentan, which is located in a valley (Carentan is actually 300 meters above the valley), we met a company of Germans being chased out of Carentan by the 101st Airborne Division that was attacking the town from the south. It was this skirmish that resulted in the death of Lt. Hutchenson of B company. It was in this skirmish, referred to earlier, that we were in an artillery barrage laid down by our own artillery. I'm sure they saw movement on the hill south of the town of Carentan and just assumed the movement was the enemy. They were partially correct. Today we call it "friendly fire." Believe me, there is nothing friendly about it. We were able to take cover behind some large oak trees and no one was hit by the friendly fire.

Shortly after the fire fight on the hill with the retreating Germans, we came into contact with some tanks and people from the Second Armored (American). We knew then we had made it back to the division. The first thing I said to the 2nd Armored troops was, "Do you have any extra K rations?" One of the 2nd Armored Division men threw me a K ration box. I sat down on the side of the road and wolfed it right down. I hadn't had anything to eat for the past two days. For that gesture I have always had kind feelings toward the "Hell on Wheels," Second Armored Division.

The Company clerk had reported us missing in action. The morning of D-Day, we knew we weren't "missing in action." We also knew we weren't A.W.O.L. because we had the company commander with us.

We joined Company C and the 501st again. and then we went into a defensive position with the 101st Airborne Division for couple of weeks, awaiting our return to England. We were in Normandy for a total of 35 days, facing the enemy on a daily basis, before we returned to our home base in England, to prepare for the Holland jump.

>S/Sgt Guy Sessions
>Company C, 501st P.I.R.
>101st Airborne Division

Chapter 17

The Pastures of Death Revisited

You don't fight the fellow rifle to rifle. You locate him and back away. Blow the hell out of him and police up.

For ten days after the route and defeat of the German 6th Parachute Infantry Regiment at Carentan, the 501st Parachute Infantry Regiment remained in a holding position commanding high ground near Le Billionaire. Day and night patrols were sent out to determine if the German infantry was moving through our area-in strength, as they retreated from Utah, Omaha, and June Beaches.

During these missions, the 501st Parachute Infantry Regiment rotated each of its three exhausted battalions, one at a time, into a rest area near Basin-A-Flot, north of Carentan. It was a peaceful area with high ground bounded by rows of Poplar trees on each side of the Escart Estuary Canal, which drained into the English Channel. I was quartered in a double shelter-half pup tent. For the first time in thirty days I was able to shower and eat K rations and British 10-1 rations in relative safety. I basked in the sun with no duties. It was far from the shooting.

While I was still in combat, I had no leisure to envision injury or death, but now I had time for such things, and I also thought about capture. Being taken prisoner would be a terrible thing, as it involves extreme personal danger, especially for the American Airborne. Of course, if you were caught with a German souvenir you would be shot. The first moments as a prisoner are perilous, as anything can happen. If you are marched about 1/2 mile into an enemy reserve area, under guard, you are safer.

Despite dealing with some bad images of combat, life in the rest area seemed quiet for awhile at Basin-A-Flot, until the German 6th Parachute Infantry Regiment, who were driven out of Carentan, got artillery range on an awards ceremony of the 101st Airborne Division in the city square and lobbed several shells. The military formation broke and sought cover. The Carentan civilians blamed us for the deaths that resulted from the bombardment.

By the end of June, after all of the 501st Parachute Infantry Regiments had been rested and rotated, we moved to St. Sauveur Le Comte for a few days, and then to coastal guard duty in the Cherbourgh port area. This gave us a few days of deluxe war scrounging, discovering ersatz coffee and canned bread.

General Taylor, commander of the 101st Airborne Division, standing on a collapsed German artillery bunker and looking down on his battle-tested veterans, congratulated them on their fine effort during Operation Overlord. He said, "You hit the ground running at the enemy. You proved the German soldier is no superman. You have beaten him on his own ground."[1]

We stood silently awaiting his concluding remarks, which we expected not to be to our liking. It was clear that we were going in again. He continued, "We have more combat for you gallant men." He was met by a sudden rush of ironic boos and cat calls.

Finally on July 19, 1944, 34 days after our first combat parachute jump, we were trucked to Veriville, where depositions were given by noncoms and jump masters against C-47 pilots who dropped us in the wrong places. We moved again, in a few days to Utah Beach, boarded LST's (landing, ship, tanks) and hours later landed at South Hampton, England. The 501st Parachute Infantry Regiment had completed all of it's first but not its last combat missions of World War II.

---

1 "You proved the German soldier is no superman."Rapport and Northwood, Rendezvous With Destiny, pge.249.

The pre-invasion warning by Axis Sally, regarding the 2000 white cemetery crosses that are waiting for us, never materialized, but things had been bad enough.[2]

I saw the debris of the storm of battle in the faces of my company friends, trying to live happily and courageously after Operation Overlord. During Operation Overlord, the 101st Airborne Division suffered a total of 4, 670 casualties and completed all of its missions. The 501st Parachute Infantry Regiment had jumped into Normandy with 168 officers and 2175 enlisted men. We returned to England having lost 213 killed in action (KIA). 590 were wounded and survived to return, 195 were missing or captured, for the total of 898 casualties, a bit over 38% of the regimental command between June 5 and July 17, 1944.[3] Some landed in the English Channel and drowned; some never left their airplane, which was hit by flak and plummeted to earth in flames; others were picked off by German snipers as they floated into flooded pastures, others jumped too late and too low with insufficient time for their parachutes to open and were killed upon hitting the ground. We were scattered widely over 60 square miles. It proved to be a strength for it confused the Germans in trying to assemble for a coordinated attack and threaten the beach landings. We engaged the enemy in skirmishes of 'cops and robbers and cowboy and Indians" battles before and after dawn on June 6, 1944.

The combat success of the 101st Airbolrne Division had been publicized in England. We were the first combat soldiers back from Normandy except for the wounded. England was a pleasant place in the summer of 1944, even at the monestary in Lambourne. We met again our recovering wounded buddies and began rebuilding our depleted platoon strength with new equipment. The combat stories that were told frightened the replacements.

Company C spread out all over England and Scotland for ten day furloughs of military mischief.

---

2 The pre-invasion waring by Axis Sally never materialized. Carl Cartlege, Unpublished Manuscript, Department of Army, <u>U.S. Military History Institute,</u> Carlisle, PA,

3 We returnrd to England having lost 213 killed in action, 500 were wounded, 195 missing or captured. Sefton, William, <u>My War,</u> pge.110.

After thirty-seven days and nights of pressing combat in Normandy, France, the aftermath of the invasion fatigue began to tell. We needed rest and recreation during a week of free time. We muddy, greasy, foul-smelling paratroopers viewed white sheets as the ultimate in luxury. We were eager to mix with the civilian population at all the '"hot Spots" to engage in civil recreation. My pockets jingled with $150.00 of back pay in coins of the realm and English paper L5 bank notes that we called "wallpaper" and "monopoly money."[4]

We were all anxious to visit London, but it had been declared off limits because it was constantly being bombed.

It was hit day and night with white phosphorous incendiary bombs by high altitude flying German Luftwaffe bombers. They flew to London, guided by the Thames River, like a swarm of maddened bees, engines pulsating angerly in unison. They came in waves every few minutes.

In spite of the nightly German Luftwaffe air raids, life in London went on with regularity as soldiers from all Allied nations acted like civilians at Rainbow Corner, Piccadilly Circus, and the many railroad stations throughout England. No matter where you went in England, you had to go through London. No matter how long you stayed you never saw it all. London was a Babel, a Mecca, the Metropolis. London was it, forever luminous.[5]

The British citizen hadn't been beaten yet, only battered. All of his cultural wealth had been dispersed throughout the English countryside for safe-keeping. His factories, supplies and children were transported to Canada. The major interior cities had a Home Guard. These were the "Minute Men" defense line to prevent the infiltration of German airborne troops.

Even though London was officially off-limits, many of our company could not resist the temptation to visit that famous city. But there were still many other wonderful places to visit all over

---

4 English banknotes we called "wallpaper" and "Monopoly Money" Gardnier, Overseas, Overpaid, Oversexed, pge.33.
5 London was a Babel, a Mecca, the Metropolis. London was it, forever luminous. Rooney, Andy, My War, pge.85.

Trial by Combat

England, and the furloughed GI's of Company C headed eagerly in all directions.

Staff Sergeants Myron G. Sessions and myself were ordered to remain in Camp Lambourne as security guards until the rest of the men returned from furlough.

Lt. Ed Jansen, Executive officer of Company C, was present every other day to write letters to families of the company combat casualties and compile "after battle reports." Myron and I decided that we had little or nothing to do daily, so we alternated days away from the camp when Lt. Jansen was absent. This scheme gave each of us two extra days of cautious freedom before the company returned from furlough.

When Myron and I finally got our furlough we decided to visit Edenborough, Scotland by the London-Midland-Scottish Railroad. We got through London as quickly as possible. But there were many short stops between London and Edenborough which slowed us. One of these stops was an overnight stay in York. Part of the evening was spent in conversation with the city Mayor about his Lincoln Zephyr. He complained that it had to be garaged because of taxes and the cost of petrol for the duration of the war. Myron and I had to suppress an urge to become sarcastic here about what a tough time he was having with this war.

When we finally reached Edenborough we spent the daylight hours sightseeing the historical sites. During the evening hours it was dancing with the Scottish "lassies" at the American USO to the music of WWII favorites such as Glenn Miller, Tommy Dorsey, and Harry James.

Upon return to Lambourne camp, Company C as well as the rest of the regiment began to receive a trickle of replacements for reorganizing, reequipping and replacing the casualty vacancies. This necessitated routine training once again. It was garrison life once more but no close order drill or manual of arms.

The deepening consequences of battle began to erupt even after our furloughs because we couldn't get out of our battle mode. It took awhile to develop our energies to full steam in the field problems. The field problems began in earnest to incorporate our Normandy successes and failures. Platoon field problems in the Cotswald

Hills horse country annoyed the English farmer when we spread out in skirmish lines, breaking down his field fences and freeing his cattle, trampling through his wheat fields, knifing the deer on private estates, and finally blowing up trout streams with hand grenades, going crazy in the English pubs with our lavish spending habits. It was difficult for us to make the transition from the slaughter and destruction of the battlefield to the quiet of the English countryside.

We had seen the enemy and destroyed him. I kept recalling images of rumbling tanks attacking German fortifications and the artillery pounding the retreating enemy infantry units as the Normandy 'break-out' got under way. I had seen how artillery shells can rip apart reinforced concrete bunkers. What these shells can do to unprotected human flesh is too dreadful to put into words.

I could not help thinking about General Taylor's statement: "We have more combat for you gallant men." His message was etched into my mind and soul. It made me determined to pour all the energies I had into mastering all of the field problems we were training for.

From time to time, during this training, we would get alerts for combat assignments. The 101st Airborne division was being considered for sixteen different airborne operations. All of them got to the paper stage and on three occasions we were sent to marshaling areas to emplane and jump on the continent.[6] Not all of the combat missions would require the mobilization of the 101st Airborne Division, some were regimental. On two of the alerts we went to Aldermaston Airdrome only to have the jumps canceled before boarding the combat-loaded aircraft.

Every time we were ordered to go in to the marshaling area, with full combat load, including ammunition, we thought it would be the real thing. We experienced a new kind of death: a death of safety and a death of innocence, a death of boredom and a death of excitement, a death again of optimism.

The world would never be the same for us. We were about to be unwilling participants in another tragedy. We now felt about war

---

6. All of them got to the paper stage and on three occasions we were sent to the marshalling area to emplane and jump on the continent. Koskimaki, George, Hell's Highway, pge.7

Trial by Combat

the way Eisenhower later expressed his feelings: "I hate war as only a soldier who has lived through it can. only as one who has seen its brutality, its futility, and its stupidity."

We soldiers had gone into battle and come out, but we knew we would have to go in again, and that all soldiers were expendable.

But as we now trained in England, we knew that, at least for us, the fighting in Normandy was over, and since this book is to be an account of that battle, I have only one more incident to relate that is associated with that battle.

As the year 1994 approached, important military and government people in America and Europe began making commemoration plans for the celebration of the 50th Anniversary of D-Day, June 6, 1944. The news media throughout the world, was reporting that old WW II American veterans who had parachuted into Normandy on June 6 were organizing and planning to plan their own way to celebrate that fateful night of soul testing. Thus was born The Return to Normandy Association. Richard Mandich, a veteran of the 506th Parachute Infantry Regiment of the 101st Airborne Division, placed an article in one of the airborne magazines calling for all veterans of the D-Day jump into Normandy to reenact that famous jump at the 50th Anniversary celebration in France.

Many responded and meetings were held at Brown Field, San Diego. We realized that this would be no easy undertaking. Many things had changed in fifty years. Those of us who were still alive had spent the postwar years trying to forget the war, trying to establish our careers, and trying to raise our families. It is a matter of record that most of us had also done what we could to make America a better country for all to live in.

Although we were no longer physically young and strong, and most of us were over seventy, our spirit was still there, and we were determined to make this memorial jump to honor our comrades who were no longer with us.

There was much opposition at first. Some were genuinely concerned that we old decrepit guys would break our brittle bones, or maybe even be killed. Some people thought we were just glory seekers, and others seemed to be jealous that we might take center stage at the D-Day ceremonies.

187

Most people, though, were enthusiastic about our project, and soon we were able to rally support. We built political fires around each objection, and finally the President of the United States gave his permission. The blessings of the French quickly followed. Nearly every nation promised to send delegations to the Anniversary ceremonies.

We began to receive world-wide publicity. Continental airlines volunteered to give us free transportation to France. The U.S. Army provided us with Ranger training at Carpequet airport, and the French government secured accommodations and equipment for us. The citizens of France were especially enthusiastic about our plans.

The requirements were strict, and we had to prove them by action. We had to have an M-42 khaki combat uniform with jump boots, a physical examination, and insurance. We also had to write an autobiography. We were given three days of parachute orientation, and had to pass a safety test. Finally we were fitted with our gear.

The most challenging task was to successfully perform three parachute jumps at Brown Field, San Diego, from 3000 feet with the new parabolic parachute.

By the time we arrived overseas, our group numbered only 40 paratroopers. Thirty of these had made the D-Day jump and 10 others had distinguished themselves in combat jumps in Africa, Sicily, Southern France and across the Rhine River. All of our band were Americans except for two gallant British paratroopers and one heroic Frenchman. We were honored to have all three with us.

Publicity was intense. All media networks, staff writers and photographers followed each one of us through our three- day training and orientation by the Rangers at Carpequet Airdrome in France.

Millions of people were gathered in the vicinity of St. Mere Eglise awaiting our arrival from the sky.

We boarded two aircraft. A C-47 carried Normandy jumpers in five sticks of six each. A twin Otter carried the remaining jumpers who had combat jumps in other campaigns. The twin Otter followed the C-47 by six minutes. In our plane the men were quiet but relaxed. We were reenacting the D-Day jump and following the same flight path, but this time it would be much different. We would now be

Trial by Combat

jumping at a safe speed and altitude, there was no anti-aircraft fire, and no battle-tested enemy waiting to slaughter us. Yet, as we neared the jump zone, my mind shifted back fifty years. I heard the sound of exploding shells, and saw the hailstorm of arcing machine gun tracers coming at me like nightmarish Roman candles.

When the time came to jump, I stepped forward to the door. Jumping #1, I led the 3rd 'stick' out the door at 4000 feet into the overcast windy sky. After an extended free fall in the dank, misty air, the opening parachute jerked me upright, and I began to oscillate under the blossoming canopy. I maneuvered my chute into a slower descent in turns, to avoid the buffeting winds. I was heading for the green pastures at twenty miles an hour. I wondered why it was taking so long until I realized that we had jumped this time at 4000 feet instead of the combat height of 350 feet.

No other jumpers were near me. I picked my landing spot at 50 feet and made a soft landing in three feet of pasture water. Three angry Normandy bulls, trying to protect their territory, approached me like a German ambushing patrol with their heads down ready for action. For a brief moment I felt helpless, the way I had felt when a second lieutenant who made me live bait so he could kill a German sniper. Three gendarmes, seeing my plight, rushed forward, splashing mud, to rescue me and bag my parachute. The bulls followed us, churning the pasture water as we crossed an electrified fence into the cheering crowd. We entered the safety net of the grandstand after a short fast boat ride in the Mederet River. The other members of the Return To Normandy were just arriving, wet and muddy, led by a bagpipe player from our group playing "Amazing Grace." The French citizens were ecstatic. They had come out to pay homage to the old *Ancienes* performing their duty once more.

We were the center of attention as we formed-up to march into Ste. Mer Eglise, ten kilometers down the same road that had seen so much fighting 50 years ago.

The size and enthusiasm of the citizens increased every kilometer as 40 of us old jumpers passed military monuments of an earlier era. The march to Ste. Mer Eglise was marred slightly by some uninvited German Paratroopers of the 6th German Parachute Regiment, our former enemy, who were standing under their banner, firing a canon salute every two minutes and singing their national anthem. The last time they fired shots at us was when we crossed their defense line at Carentan. It was a different kind of excitement for them now as they carried out ceremonial cannonading in tribute to their dead comrades. We ignored them.

The jump was an outstanding success. We were held captive in solemn French ceremonies in Ste. Mer Eglise.

The tumultuous outpouring of appreciation and admiration was a wonderful experience for us old warriors. We enjoyed all the adulation and accepted it gratefully, but with a measure of sadness as we thought of all our comrades who were no longer with us.

In the late afternoon of June 7, 1994, I visited the cemetery at Colleville Sur Mere. My face was wet with tears as I walked by row upon row of white crosses, and my thoughts went back to the horrific events during the days and nights in the Normandie battle ground. My mind was flooded with images of combat: the fire fight at Peneme, Robert J. Kahoun crumpling to the ground after being hit by a German sniper, me making my way through an enemy minefield, me huddling in a shallow ditch as artillery shells exploded all around, seeing Frank Ficarrota, who had courageously volunteered to go for ammunition, tumbling down a hedgerow embankment after being killed instantly by an unseen enemy. I also thought back to the early hours of June 7, 1944, when three of us fought off a German patrol, and they left off one of their wounded lying less than twenty yards away out in the darkness. We could hear the gurgling sounds he made as he slowly died. One of my men, who could stand the sounds no longer, crawled out and finished the poor devil off with a trench knife.

Such images occur to me often, but never as vividly as when I Walk through a military cemetery. I suppose it is so with most combat veterans, and I wonder if they all are haunted by the same question that comes into my mind all too frequently. It is a question to which their probably is no answer: Why am I still alive while so many others were killed fighting in the same battles I fought in? I wonder if it is true that if you look into an infrantryman's eyes, you can tell how much war he has seen.

I wish I could forget all about war, but I have been unable to erase its horrors from my mind. Even after all these years when I am driving along in my car and enjoying the countryside, I find myself wondering where would be the best place for my men to position their machine guns. Perhaps Plato was right when he said that only the dead have seen the end of war.

This closes my account of the Battle of Normandy, but my teeming brain is still cluttered with memories of other battles: Operation Market-Garden, Holland; the fighting around Bastogne during the Battle of the Bulge; Alsace-Lorraine sector fighting; and Austria/Yugoslavia, where the Germans were making their last stand. If God grants me the time and energy, my next volume will be about these campaigns. As that old hymn says: "Silently I wait for thee. Ready my God thy will to be."

Thomas M. Rice

Return To Normandy Association, June 6, 1994,
We jumped on the Amfrieville, France, 82nd A/B Drop Zone

Trial by Combat

Thomas M. Rice, interviewed by Brian Rooney of KTLA-TV, June 5, 1994, La Barquette Locks, Carentan, France

C47

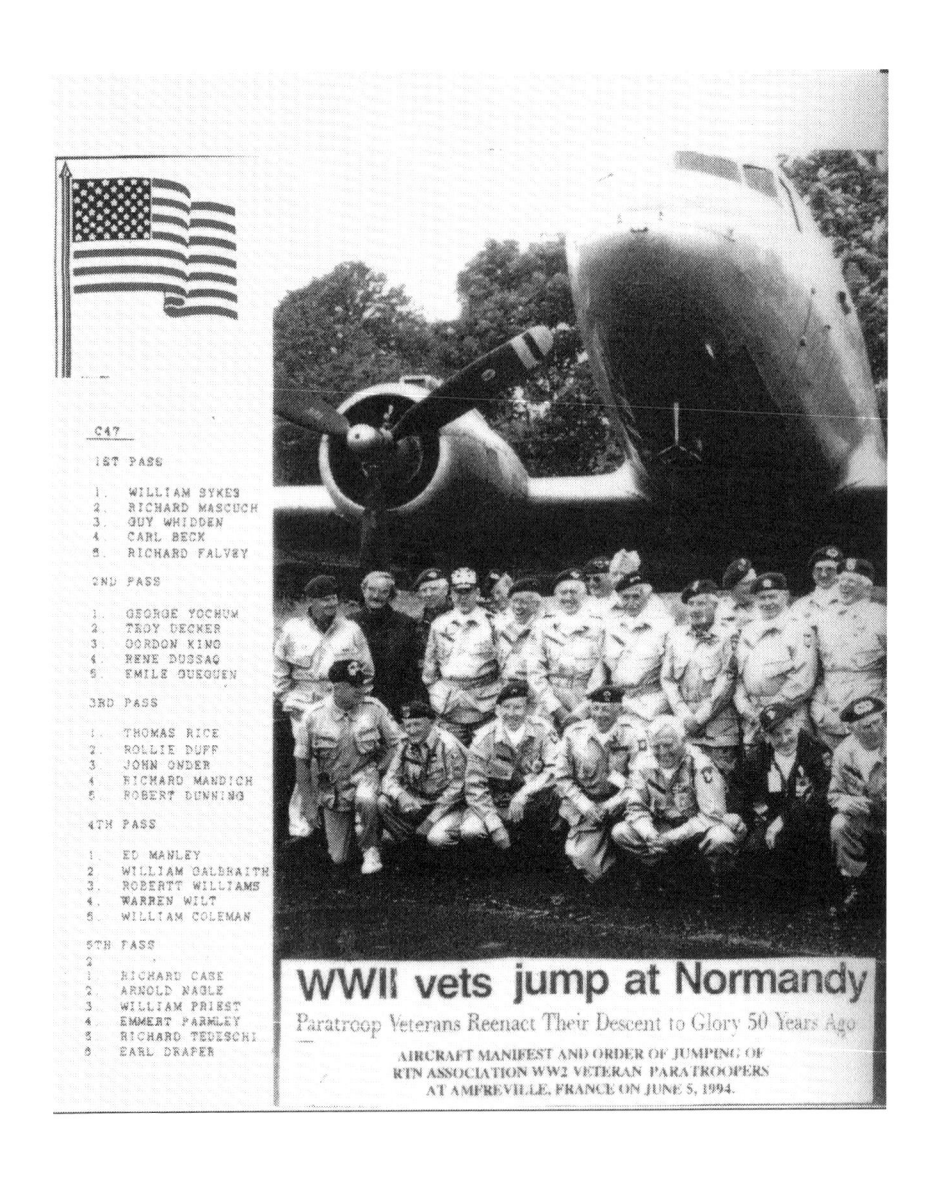

1ST PASS

1. WILLIAM SYKES
2. RICHARD MASCUCH
3. GUY WHIDDEN
4. CARL BECK
5. RICHARD FALVEY

2ND PASS

1. GEORGE YOCHUM
2. TROY DECKER
3. GORDON KING
4. RENE DUSSAQ
5. EMILE GUEGUEN

3RD PASS

1. THOMAS RICE
2. ROLLIE DUFF
3. JOHN ONDER
4. RICHARD MANDICH
5. ROBERT DUNNING

4TH PASS

1. ED MANLEY
2. WILLIAM GALBRAITH
3. ROBERTT WILLIAMS
4. WARREN WILT
5. WILLIAM COLEMAN

5TH PASS

1. RICHARD CASE
2. ARNOLD NAGLE
3. WILLIAM PRIEST
4. EMMERT PARMLEY
5. RICHARD TEDESCHI
6. EARL DRAPER

WWII vets jump at Normandy

Paratroop Veterans Reenact Their Descent to Glory 50 Years Ago

AIRCRAFT MANIFEST AND ORDER OF JUMPING OF
RTN ASSOCIATION WW2 VETERAN PARATROOPERS
AT AMFREVILLE, FRANCE ON JUNE 5, 1994.

Trial by Combat

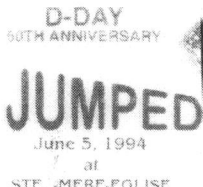

D-DAY
60TH ANNIVERSARY

JUMPED
June 5, 1994
at
STE.-MERE-EGLISE
NORMANDIE, FRANCE

TWIN OTTER

1ST PASS

1. EVERETT HALL
2. JAMES RIZZZUTO
3. AL SEPULVEDA
4. HOWARD GREENBERG
5. FREDERICK BAILEY

2ND PASS

1. ELSWORTH HARGER
2. JOHN DUNN
3. WARREN LEVANGIA
4. THOMAS ZOUZAS
5. KELLY STUMPUS

3RD PASS

1. LEE HULETT
2. KEN KASSE
3. KEN SHAKER
4. ERNEST RAXTOR
5. DURWARD REYMAN

John Onder

Thomas M. Rice

Thomas M. Rice, Camp Toccoa Memorial,
Toccoa, GA, reunion 2001

Trial by Combat

St. Mere Eglise, France,
D-Day Celebration, June 5, 1994

Thomas M. Rice

Thomas M. and Barbara Rice, Agoura, CA, 2002

Trial by Combat

Thomas M. Rice, Practice jump, for D-Day 50th Anniversary, Brown Field, Chula Vista, CA, second jump

Bibliography

Ambrose, Stephen, <u>Band of Brothers, E Company, 506 Parachute Infantry Regiment, 101 st Airborne Division, From Normandy to Hitler's Eagle Nest, 1992,</u> Simon & Schuster, New York, pgs.335..

Ambrose, Stephen, <u>D -Day, June 6, 1944, The Climatic Battle of World War II,</u> 1944, Simon & Schuster, New York, pgs. 665.

Bando, Mark, <u>The 101 st Airborne Division at Normandy,</u> 1944, Motor books International, Osceola, Wisconsin, pgs.106.

Cartledge, Carl, <u>Autobiography,</u> United States Army History Institute, Carlisle, Pennsylvania, pgs.25.

Carroll, Paul, <u>Invasion, Theyr'e coming,</u> The German Account of the 80 Days Battle ForFrance, E.P.DuttonCo, NewYork, N.Y., 1963, pgs.288, translated by E.Osre.

Critchell, Laurence, <u>Four Stars of Hell,</u> 1947, A Jove Book, BerkeleyPublishing Group, New York, pgs. 318.

Belfield, Eversely & Essame, H., <u>The Battle fot Normandy</u>, Pan Books, 1983, London, ps.256.

Fussell, Paul, <u>Doing Battle,</u> Little Brown, 1996, pgs.310.

Ganter, Richard, <u>Roll Me Over In The Clover,</u> Ballantine, 1977, pgs. 397

Gardier, Juliet, <u>Oversexed, Overpaid, Over here,</u> 1992, Canopy Books, Abbeville Press, New York, pgs. 224.

Harrison, Gordon, <u>United States Army in World War II, The European Theater of Operations, Cross-Channel Attack,</u> 1950, Konecky&Konecky, CT, 519 pgs.

Kennet, Lee, <u>G.I. The American Soldier in World War II, 1939 - 1945,</u> pgs.263.

Koskimaki, George, <u>D-Day With The Screaming Eagles,</u> 1970, 101 st Airborne Division Association, Sweetwater, Tennessee, pgs.431.

McManus, John C. <u>The Deadly Brotherhood</u>, 1998, The American Combat Soldier In World War II, Ballantine Books, NewYork, pgs.400.

O'Brien, Edward R. <u>With Geronimo Across Europe,</u> 1990, 101 st Airborne Division Association, Sweetwater, Tennessee, pgs. 433.

Orfalea, Gregory, <u>Messengers of the Lost Battalion,</u> Free Press, New York, pgs. 408.

Rapport, Leonard & Northwood, Arthur, <u>Rendezvous With Destiny, A History of the 101 st Airborne Division,</u> 1948, 101 st Airborne Division Association, Fort Campbell, Kentucky, pgs. 830.

Rooney, Andy, <u>My War,</u> 1995, Random House, Essay Productions Company Inc. New York, pgs. 318.

Sampson, Francis, <u>Lookout Below,</u> 1958, 101 st Airborne Division Association, Sweetwater, Tennessee, pgs. 266.